Revelation

By Ruby French

Published by New Generation Publishing in 2013

Copyright © Ruby French 2013

First Edition

The author asserts the moral right under the Copyright, Designs and Patents Act 1988 to be identified as the author of this work.

All Rights reserved. No part of this publication may be reproduced, stored in a retrieval system or transmitted, in any form or by any means without the prior consent of the author, nor be otherwise circulated in any form of binding or cover other than that which it is published and without a similar condition being imposed on the subsequent purchaser.

www.newgeneration-publishing.com

 **New Generation Publishing**

This book is dedicated to:
Every child in the UK, who is at risk today, and every child's life -
that has been taken, stolen, or destroyed.

....and to what they might say, if they had a voice,

You have put me in the lowest pit,
in the darkest depths.
You have taken from me, my closest friends,
and have made me repulsive to them.
You have taken my companions, and loved ones, from me.
The darkness is my closest friend.
Your terrors have destroyed me.
Turn your ear to my cry.

Taken from Psalm 88

Contents

List of Illustrations	5
About the Author	6
Preface	8
'My Dolly and I'	14
'The Art of Stuffing a Cat Into a Bag'	20
'Adding Bricks to The Bag'	26
An American Predator	35
The One Hundred Views of Parents	42
James Bulger & The Bystander Effect	53
Modern Times; Communication & Online Danger	60
Social Networks: The Machiavellian Muse	67
The Government Responds to Online Safety......Badly	71
Appeasing the Public with Public Inquiries	77
The Human Cost of Trafficking	83
Global Indecency	88
The VIP's - Very Important Paedophile	96
Taking a Gamble with Gamble	103
'The Camel's Back is About to Get it's Final Straw'	113
Your To Do List	121
The, "It's Time" – Campaign	159
An Open Letter to David Cameron PM	162

List of Illustrations

Picture 1: Lesley Ann's Funeral Procession.
Picture 2: Lesley Ann Aged Ten.
Picture 3: Ann Downey, with Lesley Ann's Clothes.
Picture 4: Ann Downey, on the Moors – Looking for Shallow Graves.

About the Author

Ruby French is a Medical Writer and Private Detective specialising in Health and Communication Investigations. Her work involves decoding and jargon busting the data and presenting it to the people who matter, you, the reader. By converting this data into an understandable format she aims to inform, enlighten and instil an interest in otherwise inaccessible or anecdotal information.

She has studied healthcare for 25 years and has a Degree in Adult Nursing, a Post Graduate Degree in Cardiac and Respiratory Medicine. She is a registered Private Investigator and has an academic interest in Communication through her practice as a Neuro-Linguistic Programmer.

Two seemingly, unconnected events in her life have led to a lifetime interest in child safety that was purely an outlet for self interest, until she began to dig a little deeper, as is her nature. There she discovered a dark and very disturbing truth.

This study into UK Child Abduction is the first in the Eye-Spy Series to be published. The book is the result of a one year study into UK Child Abduction and is a free fall into its dark, seedy and often secretive world, there is no censoring of the truth or dilution of blame, in fact, it hits hard and it hits home......because it has to.

The UK is losing the fight against something it can't see, can't count, and can't measure, massive amounts of money are changing hands, children are increasingly in danger, and are missing. Some are dying, and others remain at enormous risk, whilst Governmental Promises have been broken, year on year.

It is time to speak out, time to take action and time

to ask questions, and I can't think of anyone more determined than Ruby, to deliver on all three counts.

Preface

For 20 years I have had a dream. I will call it a dream as to call it a nightmare would give it to much power, although I do wake up sweating. When I have had this dream I know I have had it, for days after my mood may be low and I am certainly out of sorts.

The dream is about losing one of my children, either because I can't find them or because they have died. To me the dream represents being overwhelmed with things to do, or things to remember and it shows up in my life when I have a lot going on at any one time. This dream I will share with you now.

I walk into a room, but the dream is all jumbled up with an experience I had in my childhood, so the room is in fact my garden shed and I am about ten years old. The shed I remember very well, an old concrete prefabricated block with a wooden door and a metal Crittle window. The outside wall had graffiti on it. Not a pleasant sight and I now remember not a very intelligent read either. In the dream I unlock the door and go inside. The shed window is crawling with blue bottles and the air smells bad. There is a cot in there and I go over to it to pull back the blanket. The baby, which could be any one of my children, is actually a small huddle of dead baby rabbits and they have been dead for a long time. I know this because when I touch them their hair falls out and it's at this point that I wake up sweating.

When I was ten years old I had a rabbit and I used to let it out each day to run free in the garden. Much to my mothers annoyance because he would bite her ankles when she put the washing out. I say he would bite her because his name was Trevor. Much to my surprise Trevor had some babies, five in total. They were white and fluffy with a grey stripe down their backs and some looked like they were wearing socks. It was winter time and snow was coming, so Trevor and babies were moved into the shed.

Something must have been going on in my life and when I spoke about it to my mother she thinks it was probably tonsillitis, as I got that a lot. What ever it was stopped me from checking on Trevor for a couple of days. She had a large water bottle and a lot of food and besides the baby rabbits were not eating food at this stage. The day that I went to check on Trevor I discovered the water bottle had frozen solid and the bowl of food was empty and upside down. I hadn't accounted for her needing more food or more bedding or that the water bottle might freeze.

Trevor was sat at one end of the hutch and in the bedding was five little rabbits, huddled together and frozen to death.

Although this event upset me greatly, I don't remember it being profound and I can certainly think of far worse things that have happened since. In hindsight, I now realise that this must have been some sort of defining moment or life lesson that has stayed with me ever since.

I didn't start having this dream until much later in my life and when I look back to when it started happening I can pinpoint it to one or two events. The most likely cause was what I believe to be the attempted abduction of one of my children.

I had my first child when I was in my late teens and it was very tough as she was born very prematurely at a time when not many early babies would survive.

She suffered a great deal in her struggle for life. Water on the brain, seizures, visual impairment and many months on and off of life support had left her with breathing difficulties, repeated chest infections and ill health. It was a daily battle to keep it all together and there seemed to be no other young mothers that I could relate to. So it was with great joy that she survived and did well enough to attend school.

Something I had to fight hard for. She of course had not idea that life was a struggle or that she had very poor vision and simple things like trips to the park were always full of heart stopping moments when she would climb to the top of the slide and then attempt to step off into thin air.

Just six months after my daughter started school, baby number two arrived and he had no such difficulties. When he was about 6 weeks old and when I had stopped arriving at school in my pyjamas, I agreed to take my daughter to the park one day after school. It was four o'clock in the afternoon on a sunny but windy day.

The park was a small one, fenced off and in the middle of a much larger park that was directly opposite my mothers house. My mum's kitchen window overlooked the parkland and she would wave from the window as she made the tea.

My daughter was enjoying the swings and decided that she would tackle the slide, baby number two was laying in his pram, warming in the sun and I sat on the bench next to him. The small amount of play equipment was fenced off all the way around and there was a gate with a self closing device to stop children running out into the busy road, that ran alongside the park.

All was going well when I became aware of a car coming down the road and it was travelling slowly. The car, a large sliver coloured Mercedes, came to a stop outside the self closing gate. What struck me as odd was that it pulled up on to the grass, all four wheels and then stopped. The car doors opened and two women got out. They were dressed very smartly in long Sarees and trouser suits with matching long scarves. I just assumed that they were not looking for the park and besides they didn't have any children with them. They were probably visiting family, or were lost and would need some help. They entered the park and the gate closed behind them as they walked slowly and calmly over to where I was sitting.

As they came over they both stopped to look in the pram. One of them commented on the baby, how beautiful he was and asked whether he was a boy or a girl. Feeling flattered I told them he was a boy and told them what his name was.

There was nothing odd about it. As they were talking to me another person got out of the drivers side of the car. This man was short and stout and wearing a suit. He came over to the self closing gate and opening it, he then leant against the gate to keep it open. There was still nothing odd about it and I assumed he was waiting for the women to return. One of the ladies then asked me if I was breast feeding the baby and I said no. She then asked me what milk formula I was using and I began to feel a little uncomfortable, but I didn't know why. The hairs on the back of my neck seemed to move. My daughter was now standing at the top of the slide and was about to step off at any moment.

The other lady was now leaning over the pram and said *"can I just pick him up?"* Before I had a chance to answer she had put her hands under him and was about to lift him out of the pram. I stood up quickly and plunged my hand down hard on my baby's leg. Gripping him at the top of his thigh I pushed him flat to the bottom of the pram. A sort of struggle broke out in which the lady now had him under both arms and was not letting him go and I had him gripped tight and pinned down in the pram, I became aware of the other lady and in my peripheral vision I could see her moving along side me. I shouted to my daughter to sit down...now, but did not look over to her to see if she did or not. I used my other arm to lean across the pram, blocking the second lady. To the lady now holding him under his arms, I looked her square in the eyes saying " *don't you dare f***ing touch him."*

At this point there was a van coming down the road and in a snap second I remarked that it was my husband coming to collect us. The woman let go and they said something to each other and began to walk away quickly towards the man, who was still stood at the gate.

When I saw them get back into the car I went over to the slide to take my daughter down. I had a pulse beating so hard in my head that I though it would explode. I looked over to my mother's kitchen window but she wasn't there. I rushed back towards her house and soon after I left to go home.

I never said anything about it although I remember passing a comment that there were some odd people in the park. I said nothing because it just didn't compute. I racked my brains for a long time after, trying to find a reason for being singled out or what I could have done to prevent it. I felt stupid, inadequate and a failure as a parent. In a childish sort of a way I thought that I might be reported or have my children taken away for their own protection. I was very young; I stopped going out alone with the children and it was shortly after this that the dream started.

This incident went on to spark an interest in me that would follow me throughout my adult life. Child abduction doesn't, as I had once thought, start with a struggle or a fight and children can easily be separated from their parents by anyone with skill, confidence or a plausible story. Throughout my adult life and still to this day, if I hear that a child has been abducted, I need to know how. I already know why, but it's the 'how did they manage to do that?' that I have to know more about. How is a child so easily separated from its parent and why are we as parents so easily trusting and hospitable of others?

One of the first cases that I studied with interest was the 'Moors Murders' and although these murders were calculated, pre-meditated and highly violent, they are an important historical landmark in UK child abduction. The presentation of the gauntlet on stranger danger was handed to parents around the country in a stern warning that this could be their child. Parents rallied, setting up watchers for playing children and taking it in turns to arrange supervised playtimes, always bringing them home before it was dark. But somewhere along the line parents have been relieved of their duties, duped into believing that the modern world is now a much safer place. The responsibility and the risks have been diluted and it will go on to cost us dearly.

Chapter One

'My Dolly and I'

"Please, Help me, Aghh, Mum, Oh please, Please, Please...
You've got hold of my neck, I can't breathe"
Lesley Ann Downey, aged 10

This is an extract taken from the reel to reel recordings of Ian Brady and Myra Hindley recorded on Boxing Day, 1964. The transcript continues for an extraordinary length of time in which the 10 year old girl pleads for her life.... it makes a very uncomfortable read.

Lesley Anns' body was found 10 months later in a shallow grave. The fourth victim of the serial killing couple; she had unwrapped her Christmas presents just twenty four hours before; a nurses outfit, a doll and a sewing machine.

It was after the abduction of Lesley Ann Downey that the parents of 1964 became much more vigilant "don't talk to strangers" became the phrase of warning for the times. Handed to them by a police force that struggled to comprehend the magnitude of violence against the child victims.

Five months after her disappearance Lesley Ann's mother gave an interview to a reporter in which she said;*"I just hope that if she has been abducted that it was by some childless couple, who would take care of her, love her"*

The story of The Moors Murders was covered by a young reporter for the local evening news, Robert Wilson, he followed the case from the start and sat in the courtroom everyday until its end. It was a case of such graphic proportions, the photographs, the recordings and the then, cold, lofty arrogance of the couple that had carried out the ghastly crimes. As recorded in his book 'Devils Disciples' Robert Wilson is privy, first hand to the enduring pact between Hindley and Brady that would see them drip feed the case with a succession of gory details that went on to span three decades.

The combination of Brady's Nazi obsession and Hindley's strong physical build would form a bond in which she would change from local babysitter and head of the netball team to a masculine figure dressed in Nazi style apparel of high cut black leather boots and long coats. Nicknamed 'Hess' after the pianist because it made her sound more German, more Nazi, and a disciple of Hitler. She detached from her family, even breaking the bonds with her much loved younger sister, to move in with Brady. He would sing German marching songs, adorn their abode with pictures of his Nazi heroes and recite German poems whilst photographing his lover in pornographic poses.

The day that Lesley Ann was unwrapping her nurses costume, Brady and his now mesmerised lover were donning their Nazi outfits and planning to abduct a child.

The torturous case took its toll on the victims families, police officers broke down, some had to resign from their posts...and then there were the photographs that captured the nations mood. The crowds attending Lesley Anns' funeral were reminiscent of that of a monarchs procession, the photo of Lesley Ann herself – A beautiful child, round faced, with thick, brown, shoulder length curls, smiling with her head to one side like a Mancunian Shirley Temple- and the unforgettable and poignant stills of Ann

Downey, Lesley Ann's clothes clutched tightly in her hands; she is distraught and vacant with hollow eyes that look far into the distance and see nothing. She is captured again, later, by a photographer, as she stands alone on a high mound of grass overlooking the search party digging for shallow graves on the moors. At 34 years old, she is strikingly attractive and looks out of place in this picture, like an actress, on the set of a horror film.

Lesley Ann had been visiting a travelling fair that Boxing Day teatime. It had begun to get dark and her friend and her brothers had already left for home. No one knows what kept the 10 year old out longer, maybe it was the music, the bright lights or the smell of the fair; after all she was only 200 yards from her home. Then she met a childless and no doubt charming couple, also enjoying the fair.

Lesley Ann was well cared for and the only daughter of Terry and Ann Downey, much loved and doing well at school, a popular 10 year old with many friends and an interest in making dolls clothes. Lesley Ann didn't make a mistake that day, she just didn't get the signals to be afraid. The transcript of her desperate, final moments depicts this. She continually pleads with her abductors whilst interjecting her pleas with questions; "what are you doing?", "why are you doing that?", "please don't do that to me". It is her final desperate pleas, fuelled by her disbelief that are so difficult. These final pleas are cut short on the reel to reel recording by the sound of her neck being broken in asphyxiation....Lesley Ann's life was extinguished.

After the murder of Lesley Ann the recordings continued; days later, in a bizarre form of trophy gathering the murderers recorded themselves talking to locals about her disappearance. These recordings are a very insightful account of a 'murderers' ability to slot back into their community as though nothing had happened. Ten months later, Lesley Ann's body would be found and three more victims would follow her fate, before a breakthrough in the case. However, Ann Downey's torture was to continue; separation from her husband, and a miscarriage shortly after Lesley Ann's body was discovered in a shallow grave on Saddleworth Moors.

All of the victims of The Moors Murderers had desperately poignant stories and their families suffered an injustice equal to that of Lesley Ann's and her family.

The book by Robert Wilson is a very interesting and respectful account of all of those affected. Lesley Ann's story is one example chosen from his very heartfelt account.

In a case that gripped the nation many recommendations were to follow but 50 years on one question still remains; *"are we any further forward in preventing crimes of this magnitude happening to our children?"*

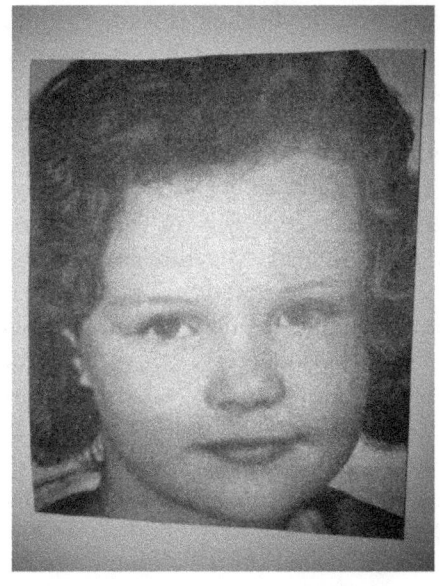

Chapter Two

'The Art of Stuffing a Cat Into a Bag'

The Art of Stuffing a Cat Into a Bag

If we look at the published figures that relate to the risks posed to our children in today's society, we might conclude that the UK has taken positive steps towards protecting them; but what if these figures are wrong? What if they don't tell us the full story? and what could possibly be the benefit of withholding such information?

The protection of children is a multi-million pound industry and one that as UK tax payers; we all contribute to.

As parents, our ability to calculate the risks to our children are reliant solely on being given the right information. This closely guarded information is exchanged between agencies of 'the industry' and is seemingly given out on a 'need to know basis'. Getting to the core of this information has proved more than difficult and has involved undercover investigation; the pressing of the industry via The Freedom of Information Act (2000) and by asking some very direct questions, such as; "where has all the money gone?"

This book is a written account of that investigation, an investigation that would seek to answer the question "what are the risks that our children face in today's society?" An investigation which aimed to convert the raw data into public knowledge and a bringing together of all the anecdotal evidence that when harmonised would make it easier for parents to read, understand and act on. This study is presented in this way to break through in a society saturated with daily events, cases and evidence that has lost its ability to evoke a reaction.

The search for answers started a year ago, but, in reality the search probably started twenty years ago, in a park in North West London. Seeking out the answer to the question on risks that when it came, would be a truly shocking revelation.

This book is about that 'need to know information' and of one thing I am sure.......

"YOU REALLY NEED TO KNOW"

When I finally got the answers to the questions that were keeping me awake at night; I sat for a couple of days in shock, paralysed by the implications that were now starring me in the face. I was not able to simply provide you with them. Not without seeking further explanation, not without seeking-out experts in the field to collaborate with and provide you with some strategies. As this is something you will undoubtedly need, when you too, realise that the responsibility to protect your children lies solely with you and that this truly mammoth task is getting tougher by the day.

So my first advice is this......put your children to bed, count them, kiss them and then pour yourself a stiff drink as you read on; you might not thank me straight away.... but you really do need to know.

What are the risks to our children in Today's society?

It's very normal in today's society that to measure something you first have to define it. You have to name it. An example would be poverty; the UK has to define poverty in order to be able to measure it. Other examples might include world hunger, cancer, or depression. If you seek to evaluate a risk on something you have to be able to count it. In order to count it; those counting it have to understand the definition of what is being counting and create a code for it. Statistics are then produced. There may be variables around the subject that require a different code in order to eliminate them and create a true account of what exactly is being counted. Again an example might be the number of 14 -16 year-olds taking exams in secondary education. These figures then go on to inform league tables. Which postal districts, county's or states are performing to the best of their ability. We see this reported all the time; which hospitals provide the best treatment and which schools produce the best exam results.

As parents we understand that if we send our child to a school undergoing special measures that we might not actualise the education we actually want for our child. Families move house in order to secure school places for their children. This is not a decision they take lightly but it's a decision they base on the information they are given. We are able to make these decisions, based on the information provided to us and we have to place a certain amount of trust in these statistics.

So ask yourself the first of many questions that will be raised in this book; If you sent your child to a secondary school that in your child's final exam year said; *"actually we had no right to produce those statistics because they were not true, but we are unequivocally sorry about your child's poor future prospects"* would you be more than a little angry? …. or is that putting it mildly?

In my day job I have, on occasion, had the unenviable task of telling a parent that their child has died. I soften the blow of course but what I am actually saying is that their relationship with their child is over …...finished.... extinct.... never going to be again....dust. Imagine all their hard work... the sleepless nights...coaching them...maths club...all those nights singing the times tables...learning spellings...the

Christmas plays where they had two lines that you had to wait an hour to hear them say; not to mention the costumes... your best pillowcases and tinsel... birthday parties.. sleepovers and later in their life the Accident and Emergency Department three weekends in a row.. or maybe that was just my boys. Nevertheless a life extinct is the hardest pill a parent ever has to swallow the biggest Knock down to get up from and some parents just don't ever get up again.

So it's not without good reason that calculating risks becomes a parental skill that is so ingrained in us that it goes on unnoticed. We calculate risk on the data available to us and without it, we are disarmed. Equally we live in a culture where we expect risk to be calculated for us. If we sign our children up to a swimming club, we expect that someone has risk assessed the swimming pool, the instructor and the facilities. We do not expect that our children will be electrocuted by the vending machine or catch Legionnaires Disease from the showers... someone else has done this for us and really the worst we can expect is the odd verruca or lost swimming cap.

So how is it possible, that in a modern society such as ours, that parents better understand the risks of washing their children's clothes above 40 degrees, than they do about the risks to the people that wear them? as soon as those clothes are put on and go off out the door; the risk of them never coming back again is actually higher that we can imagine. Yes, I know we do need to save the ozone layer but not at the cost of other more important and more immediate risks.

So if you sought the answer to the question; "what is the risk of my child being abducted by a total stranger?" And the answer came back as 1 in 59; would you, like me, reach straight for the phone and ring them? **"hello just checking on you dear...oh you're at the swimming club.... DON'T USE THE VENDING MACHINE!!!!"**

When I heard this statistic my response was; No...that's a mistake.....surely.... that just can't be right.... 1 in 59...Or 20 in every average secondary school...No.

Well, the answer as it turned out was incorrect and the reality as I was soon to discover was far, far, worse....Less than 1 in 59 in fact.

Today's risk of your child being abducted by a total stranger could be as high as 1 in 50

In one report, 1 in 59 children between the ages of 1 – 18 will experience a form of attempted abduction... and, 1 in 605 children aged between 1 – 18 will experience an actual abduction by a complete stranger and these figures by there own admission are a **gross underestimate** of the true risk.

Even more worrying is that no one has been made solely responsible for recording this data, so it isn't recorded. Why? Well, this is the important bit; there is no recognised or agreed definition of child abduction in the UK. Each police force or local authority record their data in their own way, no one asks for the data and so, they don't need to report it...**are you SHOCKED? ......Hmmm.... Sorry, but we've only just begun, better get yourself another drink!**

Nine years ago the Home Office conducted a study on the extent of Child Abduction in the UK. Of the 768 incidents recorded 56% (447 cases) involved abduction by a complete stranger. My study, a further investigation of these figures revealed a far more shocking reality.

The risks to our children are in fact far greater than we know. Furthermore the risks have been known for a long time. What could possibly be the reason of not telling us? Perhaps it was a study, carried out for the government, that suggested revealing the true scale of the problem could go on to cause a 'moral panic' and even long after this idea was abandoned by the government, the trend to keep us from the real dangers has continued.

No one is telling us, No one is responsible for recording the data.

Nothing constructive or measurable is being done, at a parental level.

Nearly ten years on and further investigation would reveal that the crimes that do get recorded are recorded incorrectly, none of the data is then shared, statistics published by the Home Office are incorrect, and the multi-million pound industry that is 'child protection' is getting it wrong..........very, very wrong.....but Why?

Chapter Three

'Adding Bricks to The Bag'

Adding Bricks to the Bag

To understand the risks, we must first understand the problems of which there are many. In an extensive list of problems here are the facts;-

FACT: There is no UK Definition of Child Abduction

There is no UK definition of child abduction, Not one of the many organisations involved in child protection, receiving public funds or claiming to inform parents about the risks, has a working definition. There just isn't one, and there never has been one. For a short time we looked to the American definition but this has problems of its own. America defines child abduction as;

> *"a stranger or slight acquaintance perpetuates a non-family abduction in which the child is detained overnight, transported at least 50 miles, held for ransom, abducted with intent to keep the child permanently, or killed" (Sedlak et al, 2002)*

The problem being that as evidence suggests, most child abductions do not involve transporting the victim for 50 miles or more, and that half of all those children actually abducted are not intended to be kept overnight; and are often killed within 3 hours of being taken. Further studies as far back as 1992; also suggest that an inability to define child abduction has serious repercussions for both informing public debate and any development of effective prevention and safety measures.

We can all appreciate that not having a working definition does make it difficult, but 20 years on we are still no further towards achieving one. Imagine all Doctors stating that they were no longer going to treat or report on Diabetes any more because there wasn't an adequate working definition. It just wouldn't happen, society wouldn't stand for it.

There has to be another reason for not agreeing a working definition, could it be that with a working definition, that the crime statistics would then need to be recorded nationally, and that the infrastructure to record them just isn't in place?

FACT: There is no Single Method of Recording Child Abduction

The year on year data shows a decline in child abduction as a whole. Not because child abduction has lessened or because we have foiled it, but rather because there is no reason to report it. The crime can be counted however, if it is recorded as a serious offence or a rape instead, and will contribute to a different league table. Those league table statistics then; can not be drilled down into ages, offences, or severity...the data is simply lost.

None of the agencies collaboratively exchange or discuss their data. There is no national register or single point of recording for this nationwide crime.

So the reality is there is no actual figure of child abduction in the UK and the figures of 1 in 59, were actually chosen from a study, to represent only those crimes that are reported correctly and held on a computer somewhere. They are at best, by their own admission, misleading.

This is the extract from the report 'Taken' and it refers to figures requested from police forces around the country. The problem was further compounded by the fact that not all of the police forces acted on the request. They didn't supply any figures, presumably they were not being obstructive, they had not recorded them so, they just didn't have them.

"These figures are a poor indicator of the actual level of child abduction, by a stranger, in the UK. Gallagher et al (2008) indicate that at least one in 59 children will experience some form of attempted abduction by a stranger, in the course of their lifetime. At least one in 605 children will experience an actual abduction by a stranger." Taken, 2012

The study figure appears to have been taken and applied to the population as a whole. The study has its critics, in that it was carried out in a single part of the country and did not represent the more densely populated areas, such as London.

But in reality, that would just make the risk higher.

These figures are used to represent those crimes that are firstly, the ones that get reported, and secondly, those that are entered correctly. If there is a chance of apprehending the person responsible then they are recorded as a Rape or Serious Assault...presumably to obtain a conviction; This is use of the principle crime rule.

Equally, you could not prove abduction if you do not have a definition by which to measure it.

FACT: The Abduction Law stops at 16 years old despite the over 16s being one of the highest at risk categories; so they are not recorded.

The law in England stops at the age of 16 years when applied to a child whom has been abducted but the law states that a child is a child until the age of 18. One of the highest at risk groups for abduction are girls aged between 13 – 17 years old and of those abducted this is the age group and gender most likely to be killed. The reason for not recording these crimes as an abduction is that if the abduction results in a rape or murder then again the 'principal crime rule' applies.

FACT: The estimated annual costs of missing children in the UK is £222m (2010)

We need to understand these figures as they relate to the police costs and do not reflect the wider cost to society, such as health, education and the cost of prosecution. Over a five year period (2003-2008) the police costs to support missing persons (child) cases was just under £500m. This is an extraordinarily large amount of money and it is rising, year on year. This figure also fails to include the annual cost of child abuse which the NSPCC estimated was 12 Billion pounds in the UK, in 2007. Many services and responses overlap or have blurred boundaries and their responses appear to be disorganised and lacking in direction or leadership. A further study by Action for Children compared the cost of tackling social problems in 16 different countries – from this, they were able to estimate that the cost to the UK, of not adequately addressing its social problems is estimated to be 4 Trillion Pounds over the next 20 years. The cost of services that fail to tackle the problems of 'Missing Children' in a timely and responsive way, is a huge drain on our society and our public purse is haemorrhaging funds in a bid to keep up. Make no mistake about who's bill this is. It is ours and it will continue to cost us dearly.

FACT: More is Known on the Type of Risk That we Should Warn Young Children and Their Parents About, but Nothing is Being Done.

The vast majority of abductions occurred when a child was without an adult. The victims of these crimes had an average age of 12 and three quarters were girls.

Two thirds of the attempted abductions by a stranger were carried out by someone in a car, getting out of a car, or attempting to pull the child into their car. This is known, but do parents know it? Our findings suggest that they don't. Have we had any warnings about stranger perpetrated crimes on young girls? How many young girls do we see every day after school, walking alone? How many school buses had their route taken out of service last year? They will probably be unequivocally sorry about that too. Nearly half of all the victims report being grabbed, dragged or held to the point that they had to struggle to get free.

Shall we add 'teaching younger children the best way to escape from a stranger' to the national curriculum? No.... from the new buzz of a child centred perspective, they would rather play tag rugby because it's too cold to play real rugby so they can just tuck an old tea towel in their pants and run around the school hall, in moronic circles. If you have ever witnessed this disorganised mass squeaking of trainers, you would have to agree that an hour spent teaching children skills that could be transferred to the real world would be time better spent. It would still be a physical activity. Sorry, if there is anyone out there with a Masters Degree or a PHD in Tag-Rugby, I didn't mean to offend.

FACT: Nobody Knows how Effective Prevention is or Whether any of the Messages are Actually Getting Through to Parents or Their Children; it Just Isn't Measured!

The report highlights that what is being done, may not be effective. It is not known how well it is accessed or what, if any effect it has. This is largely affected by the fact that none of it is tested or measured. This is the equivalent of a leaflet drop campaign, where the person responsible for delivering the leaflets decides to chuck them away because nobody is checking on him.

Targeting a group that is saturated in information overload is a campaign on a 'hiding to nothing'. I have managed to find one strategy about online safety.....and I have to say it was dull.

Surely we can do better than that? No child or adult would access this information. I had to search for it, download it, print it, and then it used half of my printer ink when I had to print 26 full colour photographs of people or models pretending to be the average family, all sitting together and discussing the internet.

That wasn't necessary. Quite frankly I could do better and so could they. I will look at these documents again because they make some extraordinary claims for what has actually been achieved.

FACT: Crimes are not recorded because we have the wrong kind of software"

This was an issue highlighted by the Bichard Inquiry and relates to the ability of police services to both record and access information stored on a single system.

This information could be accessed by any police force wanting to cross reference a person that they may be suspicious about or have held in their custody. Of the 43 police forces that had requests for 'Missing Children' data, only 37 replied. The CEOP reported that the data that was supplied did not adequately record the incidences and disparity in recording crimes was widespread. Bichard, who has a responsibility to revisit his inquiry, on a six monthly basis, has made clear his disappointment that the recommendations for a single method of recording child crime is still not a reality. The original plan, back in 2004, was to go with the programme – IMPACT.

However, this was rejected as unworkable when it failed to deliver on a number of key aspects. Namely, it could not monitor crime, as had once been thought. The programme had been set to replace the multi-systems in place across UK police forces and needed to address all aspects of police work. The IMPACT programme then considered CRISP – The Cross Regional Information Sharing Project - yet another system hailed to deliver. The promise of CRISP was the ability to share information among police forces in a timely and responsive way. Not all police forces are using this system and if they need information from it, they then need to ring a force that is using the system, and put in a request. The cost of the system that promised to meet the recommendations of Bichard, at the time of his report in 2004, was £163million pounds. It became more evident, at a later date, in one of Bichard's six monthly reviews, that this computer system would not meet the required specification, the cost to meet the original specification had suddenly changed to £367million. To date, neither system is operational and cases such as the most recent Ian Watkins, lead singer of Lostprophets, can be our acid test.

FACT: Attempted Abductions are on the Increase but Nobody Knows Why.

Attempted abduction is on the rise and this is impart responsible for our high rate of attempted abduction figures. Why this is happening is not known, some theories suggesting that they are 'practice attempts' by paedophiles, prior to their first actual abduction. There were no statistics relating to the number of attempts perpetrated by convicted paedophiles. It simply wasn't recorded. But we know from the case files of Millie Dowler that this is certainly the case and convicted paedophiles have several attempts at abduction, before becoming successful in their ability to commit sexual crime. Another theory is that children are more adept at escape. Whilst I would like to believe this theory, my investigation would suggest that this is not the case. Equally, this would not account for the rise in attempted abductions when there is a known reduction in the self-report of attempted abduction. One explanation that we have to consider, is the activity of gang-related opportunistic crime. This is certainly on the increase and may be responsible for the rise in car-perpetrated attempts. There is a need for further investigation or research into the reasons behind increased attempted abduction, and this certainly builds a case for better national crime recording in the future.

FACT: It's Our Own Fault That we Don't Know the Risks Because we will Just Panic.

The report highlights the effect of the media in a decision to keep us in the dark. As the risk to our children (presuming they could measure it in the first place) would be too high, in affecting their development, socially, psychologically and physically.

"Some commentators have seen evidence of child abduction forming part of a moral panic', creating increasingly paranoid parents." from Taken, 2012

So, in other words, we just wont tell parents the real risk in the hope that they will continue living a normal life and if something goes wrong we will just tell them how 'unequivocally' sorry we are" Although the view on moral panic is criticised as an outdated view, this trend has continued. The theme now is to address the problem from a child centred understanding of the risk. Now I might be splitting hairs here, but how are children to understand the risks? Surely children take their lead from their parents (who are not risk aware) these parents can then be blamed for being absent minded, feckless and a lost generation. As parents we cant win, we are damned if we do let out our "latch-key children" and damned if we don't – Its our fault if our teenager becomes obese and cant run a mile".

Question
" If these figures are wrong then can you, just give us the real-risk data?"

Chapter Four

An American Predator

An American Predator

In July 2013, an American Cable Channel carried out an experiment to see how many children would follow a complete stranger out of a park. The experiment revealed that despite the children's parents being close by, 35 percent of the children left the park and went with the would-be predator. These children had been primed with "you never talk to strangers" and the familiar parental input on stranger danger. But as the experiment got under-way, it became evident that these boundaries were not at all adequate or robust.

The important part of the experiment is recognising the rationale that the children gave when recalling why they had gone with a complete stranger. The experiment involved twenty children and each was staged to play in a park area that was a fenced off or protected zone. Their parents were also sat within visible sight and the children were given the instruction to play, returning to their parents if they needed them.

The pretend predator was dressed in normal clothing and entered the park where the children were playing. He was carrying a puppy and set down near the play area. All the children in the experiment came over to the stranger and petted the puppy. The predator used the puppy as his reason to leave the park. He told the children that he needed to give the puppy some water and that the water was in his car.

Time and time again, the children followed the predator out of the park and across a large car park to his car. One mother describes her sheer disbelief as she watched her young son leave the park, without even looking back to where she was sitting. One of the children was persuaded to try out the puppy's cage, by climbing into the boot of the would-be-paedophile's car and getting into the puppy cage, the cage was then locked. This mother watched in horror and would later say "my heart was pounding and I just couldn't believe what I was seeing".

The experiment was part of a drive to convince parents to move away from the outdated approach of 'Stranger Danger' and concludes that developing scenarios that encourage critical thinking, even in young children, is a more modern approach to the risks of child abduction. The experiment was overseen by Americas leading child psychologist Dr Rebecca Bailey, who suggests it is essential to test children and that this needs to be explored and carried out regularly, if it is to be effective.

America has a working definition of child abduction and this measure provides them with the key figures on the annual number of child abductions in the US. According to their figures 2,000 children are abducted in America, every day.

Understanding the problem from a child's perspective is key to reducing these figures both in America and the UK. In other words, we should be assessing their ability and rationale in exercises based on critical thinking.

The reasoning used by the children in this experiment is insightful when considering that all of the children chosen for the experiment were considered by their parents, to be knowledgeable on the dangers of strangers in a public place.

One child describes seeing the predator and deciding that if this person was able to care for a puppy, then he was going to be a *nice* person. Another describes his actions as "the predator didn't look like a predator". Dr Rebecca Bailey cites this reason as one of the compounding factors and suggests that many children have an outdated belief of what a predator looks like, and that the down and out, toothless person is a myth.

Of the 13 children who ran away all gave the reasons of not trusting a stranger, with one child sighting that he did not want to let his mother down.

There are an estimated 150,000 child abductions every year in the US and this figure also includes those children abducted by someone known to the child. If children already know their abductor, or have already placed trust in an individual, then the risks are far higher.

The American Child Safety Website, a single point of access for parents to obtain information about safety programmes in their area, reinforces that there are many people who want your children just as much as you do. However, these are likely to be sexually motivated. Incidentally, UK parents have been promised a single point of access for information on child safety, for a decade. The much talked about and promised 'Single Hub' just hasn't materialised.

We need to be very clear, when explaining the risks to our children as it may be difficult for them to comprehend. There has not yet been a single case reported of a child abducted because the abductor wanted to love them more. When discussing safety with our children it might be a good idea to explain why someone else might want to take them.

Is it time to talk honestly to our children, about why other people might want them just a much as we do?

How can we protect our children without scaring them? How can we give them enough information to protect themselves, without affecting their social, psychological and physiological development?

A good place to start is to understand where children are at, in terms of their beliefs, which changes, as does their abilities. First lets look at the differences and similarities on a child's ability to make an informed decision.

Children Under Seven:

Most children under the age of seven will believe mostly any self reported statement from, what they consider to be, a reliable source. They will see self report as an effective means to gather information about a certain persons characteristics.

An example would be a child asking an adult if they are good at making cakes? The adult, who may never have baked a cake in their life or may be notoriously bad at cooking, could convince a child that they are a very good baker. This self report by the adult is likely to remain unchallenged and require no proof whatsoever, in this age group.

Older children from eight years onwards become much more willing to be sceptical of self report, and will even demonstrate enough skill to cross-check another's self report, by seeking out a reliable source. This is a massive leap in what is, after all, a very short time. This high level jump is thought to occur at a time and signal their social maturity. It is however, possible to speed up this process in younger children by preparing them early. This can be achieved with the skill of 'Critical Thinking'. So how does it work?

Teaching younger children critical thinking and critical reasoning skills is highly beneficial and by using critical thinking skills they are more likely to develop faster, socially and display better self reliant problem solving abilities. The good news is that these skills can be taught at a very early age.

The differences and the similarities can be seen as this. Children who display higher or better formed critical thinking, and so therefore, will posses greater social maturity will be more sceptical of adults self report and will seek out a reliable to source to either back this up or reinforce it. They will also be able to chose a reliable source or monitor what they perceive to be, reliable characteristics. They will compare self report against peer report and teacher report or by behavioural observation. In other words - does this behaviour actually match the self report.

So, can the great cook bake a great cake? Younger children who have not had the benefit of additional learning or been raised to this level of social maturity, may conclude that self report is proof enough. They will not, then be able to draw on any correlation between self report and an ulterior motive. An example might include "as I am an excellent,weight lifter, come behind this building and watch me lift something really heavy."

Another country renowned for its early child social maturity is China and in comparison Chinese six to seven year-olds display the same level of social maturation as ten and eleven year-olds in the UK or the United States. They do this because of their culturally different, social norms. Chinese six to seven year-olds display greater social maturation because they display greater scepticism. This is due to the social experiences they retain in their cultural norms, a Chinese child will have a tendency to move away from displaying their own feelings, as this would be considered self indulgent and against their cultural harmony. So, someone outwardly displaying these characteristics, would immediately raise feelings of scepticism in the average Chinese six to seven year old. This early adoption of traditional values means that the younger Chinese child is, more socially experienced in terms of cultural norms, than it's more western counterparts.

Critical Thinking

How can we get our children to start thinking more critically? Here are some examples of dilemmas to discuss with children aged 5 to 8 years old.

What is the difference between a chickens egg, and a frogs egg?

The response: you are looking for your child's ability to reason and to deliver answers that have been through some sort of analysis, synthesis and evaluation.

This will improve with practice but their answers can be reached by breaking down the various points into parts. The language of analysis to instil in your child is task orientated skills – being able to; *analyse, explain, compare, separate, classify, or jointly arrange.* So, the question, about the eggs becomes an exercise in analysing the differences and similarities between the eggs and arranging, justifying and reporting back what the differences are and why. The question would also need to breakdown into parts the various stages, for example, the eggs shape, surface, density, colour, size and so on. Your child, once an accomplished critical thinker, could really spend all day thinking about this question.

This early pondering in the same methodological thinking displayed by Einstein or Beethoven. This advanced ability at problem solving allows children to become ultra smart and great analysts of whatever presents itself in front of them.

Synthesis applies to the child's ability to attach prior learning to the new question. This will allow the prior learning, which may be wrong, to be tested and connections are drawn between what was thought before and what is now known and tested out. Evaluation allows the child to summarize all the data and conclude a course of action that would have not been there before. Because it is inferred by them and is their conclusion, when completed critically, is likely to be both well thought out and implicitly understood.

The work books for children contain questions and themes that can rumble on for weeks and children are encouraged to compare their answers in a bid to improve their skills. The Chickens Egg and Frogs Egg Question is just a nonsense that is for practice' but imagine asking them to: Compare and contrast the abilities and achievements of the country's last five Prime Ministers, and them finding it easy. Critical thinking is the one thing that is both learned through *direct experiential learning* – I touched the egg and it was warm but the eggs surface was rough, and also *imaginative process learning* – I imagine that if I touched the egg it might be warm or cold and the surface would feel powdery.

This process, of learning the process of critical thinking, is a life skill that really accelerates your child into the world of the greats. The great thinkers, reflectors and philosophers. Their capability catapults them into being able to problem-solve at a much higher level, testing their own reasoning and tweaking as they go. Their own in depth theories will feel normal when they function at this level.

It will be one of the greatest gifts you can give them and will be reflected in their academic and lifelong skills.

workbooks at, not-for-profit prices are available from the website

Chapter Five

The One Hundred Views of Parents

The 'Over to You':100 Views Child Safety Survey Pilot

In a bid to gain some insight into the UK understanding of the risks of child abduction at a parental level, we carried out a survey pilot. One Hundred families took part in both the South East and South West of England. The sample group were chosen from a cross section of working parents, at home parents, General Practitioners, Healthcare Workers, Teachers and High Street Vendors. All were parents, all were surveyed anonymously.

The purpose of the 10 question survey was to better understand the level of known risk. What do parents believe the risk to be? What they tell their children, and where this teaching came from. Interestingly we asked the question of whether they would want to know more about the risks, if more information were available and who they felt was responsible for passing on this knowledge. We were also keen to establish what parents would do if presented with the scenario of witnessing a child abduction and whether they felt they would intervene. The aim was to obtain qualitative data on what parents believe. The results of the survey were shocking and represent the scale to which UK parents, have been let down.

The Survey Results
Question One

Using a number between 0 and 10, with 0 representing No Worries and 10 representing the Most Worried;

How worried are you about your child's safety?

The Results

Seven parents concluded that they were not worried about their child's safety.

This finding can be viewed in many different ways. This could suggest that seven of the parents have got it completely covered and do not need to worry. I find this a little hard to believe and think the question was answered in this way as these parents had no other way of equating the risks because they simply aren't known.

In fact if we take the continuum to have a mid point, we could say that the midpoint was five. So those parents rating under a five would be less worried, on average, than those rating as a five or above. Or are they? It could be that those scoring a five and below are just reacting to what is known about the risks, and in their case, this might be very little. The total number of parents rating a five or under represented 37 per cent of the sample. A further 60 per cent in the sample group scored above the midpoint.

From this data collection, we can conclude that 60 per cent of parents are worried about their child's safety in general, a further 37 per cent were not overly worried but may not be well informed and 3 percent of people did not provide legible answers.

Question Two

As a parent are you more worried about your child's
(a) online safety
(b) safety when out and about?

The Results

We then asked parents to draw a distinction between online safety and safety when out and about. The same sorts of data were returned and our worried parents in question one seem to be well represented in question two.

Question Three

If you had to answer, what do you think are the chances of your child ever being abducted by a complete stranger?

(a) 1 in 50
(b) 1 in 500
(c) 1 in 5,000
(d) 1 in 50,000

The Results

Now we asked parents about pinpointing a level of risk. This gave them four choices and the rating was supposed to represent a risk that they felt was, real, felt, or known. To either their own child, or children in general. What is interesting about this data is that there is almost an even display of risk, with a slightly higher risk in the least at risk group. Again this least likely risk group could be being bolstered by a group of parents that were not risk aware, as was represented in answer one. But we will not know this yet. However those scoring a zero on question one are analysed further at the end of the report.

Question Four

Do you talk to your child/children about Stranger Danger?

(a) Yes, I do sometimes
(b) Yes, I do often
(c) No, I leave it to the school

The Results

Next we asked parents to tell us how often they spoke to their children, in an constructive way, about 'Stranger Danger' and how often if at all, they felt they needed to reinforce it. Interestingly the parents recorded almost in equal quantities the amount of time spent teaching children on 'Stranger Danger'. It is true that the difference between often and sometimes is a subjective measure and these groups have clearly blurred boundaries I think it is positive that 95 per cent of the parents we surveyed are talking to their children about 'Stranger Danger – But is this imparting of knowledge meaningful and can we say that parents have any measure of effectiveness?

Question Five

If there was more information available about the personal safety risks to your child/children; would you, as a parent, want to know?

(a) Yes, I would want to know

(b) No, I would not want to know.

The Results

This question was clear cut and was aimed to demonstrate that despite the information being *sometimes frightening* parents do actually want to know more.

The question itself was worded in a way that represents the current situation in that more is known about the risks to our children. Do parents really want to know. The percentage of parents who did want to know was 94 per cent with a 4 percent attrition rate. This is important because there has been a trend, over a long period of time, to keep parents from the facts and figures. Remember those comments about us all being a nation of panicked parents that are not capable of doing anything constructive with the information.

Question Six

Who do you think is responsible for making sure that parents get the right information on child personal safety and prevention advice?

The Results

This question generated the most spontaneous results, parents seemed to have no difficulty in answering who they thought was responsible for disseminating the information on child safety to them and their children. The answers were a real mixed bag and in a collective sense we could say that everyone is responsible but we have to be aware of bystander phenomena and what effect the dilution of responsibility has on ensuring that the message gets delivered. The answers as you can see form the graph are in equal first, second and third, parents feel that the responsibility falls at the feet of government, schools, and parents, with only twelve percent thinking that it was a police force responsible for delivering the information.

Question Seven

Do you feel that as a parent you have the right to know how safe your child is?

The Results

This question was added to assess what parents thought they had a right to know. Many parents firmly believe that if Government are aware of a risk to children and that this risk changes over time then they absolutely have the right to know, and

I would agree.

Question Eight

If you were out and you saw a child in obvious difficulty with a group or an adult would you intervene?

(a) Yes, but only verbally,

(b) Yes, I'd tell someone or get help,

(c) Yes, I'd get involved physically,

(d) No, I'd have to walk away

(e) No, it's not my business

The Results

Would you be a Bystander?

This data was collected to assess how many of know exactly what we would do if presented with a 'James Bulger Scenario' and could the act of being asked the question make any difference? (Tartan Elephants)

How Much Does the Eiffel Tower Weigh?

Your brain stores images of all the things you need to know, example, if I asked you to recall a blue car, you will have an internal picture that you use over and over again. This may not have even been your blue car, but it is the representation of a blue car that your brain has chosen to hold on to, in its memory bank, and will be used, by you, from now until you die. It will be the image that your brain first recalls when someone speaks about, or asks you to, recall a blue car.

So, just as the brain holds onto these images, it also holds onto a plan. The plan however, has a higher chance of being a functioning plan if it has been visualised or called into play, before it is needed. This plan run-through should be done regularly and is one of the reasons we carry out fire drills and evacuation procedures. When practised, these plans become ingrained. We are, by our practice, primed for action.

Now, lets do a test, I want you to imagine the Eiffel Tower. No problem for you, this is an iconic Iron structure, known around the world. It is 320 Metres High or (1,050) feet tall. Wow! You can even imagine it's slightly brown structure in the flick of an image that first came when I asked you to imagine it.

Now I'm going to change that image you hold for evermore, after reading this section, close your eyes and imagine the image that originally flashed before you, and even with your eyes closed, you will be physically looking up to the left or the right as you do this. This is you accessing the image. Imagine it there and keep it in your thoughts. Now draw from another image, I want you to imagine one of those big iron weights the square-ish ones with a metal ring through the top that you would need to lift up if there were any attempt to lift it. Got that image? Now, imagine the writing 10,000 Tonnes painted on it, in big white letters. Look at it for a while and imagine it there with your eyes closed.

Now synthesise the image by moving it into your Eiffel Tower picture, place the weight at the bottom of the Eiffel Tower and visualise it there for a few moments.

See how it sits, how the sunlight bounces off of it and people point at it, as they walk past the tower. See the big, white, writing - read it to yourself. Okay job done, image changed and now you know that the Eiffel Tower Weighs 10,000 Tonnes. You will never need to ask anyone again, not that you really did in the first place. But it is now your image. You never know, you may just win a pub quiz with that answer one day or you might be someone's phone a friend. You can thank me later, it's fine.

Linking Mental Images with Acting Out a Plan
Question Eight Answered

The findings on this question make very interesting reading, 100 per cent of those people who answered the question, remember that three answers were illegible, have all stated that they would do something. In other words they have all stressed that they would be 'called to action' in some way. Either, to be involved physically, or verbally, or by raising the alarm.

When remembering the James Bulger Case of Fifteen adults with an opportunity to act, becoming 'bystanders' If we asked any one of them, they may well say, that they later reflected on their decision to walk away and wished they had done something differently. All humans are capable of feeling this. All of us could have got home and wished we'd done something differently. We have all had that feeling in the 'pit of our stomachs' that something may have just slipped through our fingers or fallen through the net, and it must be remembered that the ability to reflect on something and empathise, is what makes us human. But we can assist the process. By playing the process out in our minds, we are telling our brain exactly what we ought to do if faced with the problem. We are right there imaging it in a critically thought out way,

"By simply asking the question and expecting a response, we are helping that person, build a process in their mind, that can be called into action - without dilemma or question, should the need ever arise."

Critical thinking is also a skill that can be taken on at any stage in someone's life, you are just never too old to benefit. It is a gift to spend time with anyone who is truly a critical thinker. Here's a gift for you to critically analyse, synthesise and evaluate,

The best time to plant a tree was twenty years ago, the second best time was today,

The third best time has passed, what does this mean?

Answer

The third best time was now.....but now that's gone.
The fourth best time is a matter of analysis, synthesis and evaluation.

Question Nine

What were you taught about child Safety?

The Results

The ninth question and one that requires a reflective answer is interesting as it highlights the extent to which, despite progressions in knowledge being made, we have failed to move on. Or at least move away from advice that we now know is, not helpful. Most of the data included in question nine by the parents did form more than a one word answer. We have, however used the first answer to produce some statistics in this form and a greater analysis, is ongoing.

It is also interesting to note that 57 percent of parents are still using a stranger danger type strategy to warn their children about paedophiles and other on the street risk. 22 percent admit they know nothing that they can pass on and the biggest shock for us was the amount of respondents whom cited they were advising children on social networking sites. This was just 2 percent. This is one are of risk that has been heavily researched by the government and much of our 'missing funds' have been played away here. Documents that are not read or measured are claimed to have accessed 8 million children and their families. We are not seeing that evidenced here.

This is a difficult and unexpected result in terms of all of the money spent on educating families about online safety, more research is needed to find out why they are able to quote teaching the 'Green Cross Code' to their children instead of any of the multitude of online safety messages. Five families couldn't respond as they just didn't have an answer. Nothing was memorable enough to warrant an answer.

Nothing in terms of 'Click CEOP' or the 'Think U Know' campaign. Nothing, not even the recent campaign from the NSPCC – 'PANTS.' I think we have to remember that this was a very open ended question to parents and it asked them what they were taught. It had no time scale and related to parents only. In a bid to harness what they might know as opposed to what they were prepared to hand on. This could have been learnt at any point in their life, either as a child or as an adult.

Question Ten
Who taught you these skills?

The Results

This was the final question in our survey and the aim was to both find out and inform. In finding out – we wanted to know who taught our parents these skills? We suspected that a lot would claim that it was their parents. As we were talking about a generation or two away from our average six to ten year olds today. The results were largely predictable with the same number of people who were taught 'stranger danger' being taught by their parents and this seems entirely reasonable. The same amount of parents claim that nothing constructive was taught to them that they can recall as an answer. Interestingly, this figure also represents the same amount of parents whom stated that they had been taught nothing in question nine.

I think that we had some very honest parents and some very obvious opportunities to improve the imparting of data from known-by-parent and from parent-to-child.

Discussion

It is clear from the results of this pilot survey, that child safety is in urgent need of a revamp. 'Stranger Danger is not a Changer', it will not change a situation for the better and we need a radical overhaul of what we tell and teach our children.

Relying on mantra's such as The 'Green Cross Code' as an adequate means of protection, is simply not going to be enough to keep them from being harmed. The responsibility, although highlighted in the survey as - the domain of Government or Schools or others, is actually the job of parents. Yes, we may all need some guidance, but its ours. There is, however, a 'new kid on the block' and it is called Critical -Thinking, a skill for protection and a skill for life. Teaching children critical thinking is imperative to their ability to react –

appropriately and timely to the challenges that they face in a rapidly changing social landscape.

Keeping children both integrated and engaged in family life is also key to their future success. The Government needs to respond urgently to the deficits in child safety. The time in now.....we can wait no more.

Chapter Six

James Bulger & The Bystander Effect

James Bulger & The Bystander Effect

In February 1993, one of the most shocking crimes was committed against a child. A crime so heinous that the public's reaction was one of pure anger. When two 10 year old boys abducted a two year old boy from a shopping centre and subjected him to an ordeal that ended in his untimely, undignified and lonely death.

Equally shocking was the fact that a two and half hour window existed to prevent this little boys' death. The chance to prevent the crime was missed and his encounter with at least 15 members of the public who intervened still failed to prevent what was to become a catalogue of missed opportunities, by bystanders.

The crime, on reflection, is very interesting as it demonstrates perfectly the phenomena that is 'Bystander Effect' and offers us an insight into the final hours of his life. The case you may know as the unimaginable abduction and murder of James Bulger; from a Merseyside Shopping Centre, one month before his third birthday.

The two ten year old boys then named Robert Thompson and Jon Venables who gave in to police questioning; surrendered a chilling and sometimes graphic demonstration of the lengths that they went to, to commit this murder. They were approached many times and questioned by members of the public, and had ample opportunity to stop what they were doing.... but they did not. Do read on, because if you think you know this case, you may need to think again.

12th February 1993

On the morning of 12th February 1993, a nurse was setting up a health information stall in the Strand Shopping Centre and shop keepers were busy preparing to open up, on what was a midweek school day.

Later that morning in the now busy shopping centre, the nurse is discussing a health issue with an elderly lady; other people approach the stand taking leaflets or waiting in turn to talk to the nurse. A ten year old boy approached and picked up a leaflet, flicking through it he throws it back down on the stand. A second boy joins him and they begin messing about; shoving into each other, knocking into the table of leaflets and then into the elderly lady. Other people in the queue intervene telling the two boys to 'sling their hook and move on' they leave. They continued to misbehave taunting abuse and intimidating an elderly shopper and going into shops only to be asked to leave by the shop keepers.

One of the boys is seen emerging from a toy shop, he smiles to his friend and holds up a tin of modelling paint. A father, waiting outside describes seeing him pull the tin from his pocket and remarked that he was sure that the boy had stolen it.

It was now a little after lunchtime, the two boys can be seen on CCTV and it is known that they remained in the shopping centre. We know this because a separate incident would place them there at that time, but we will come back to this later.

At 15:37 James and his mother come into view on CCTV. James' mum, Denise, goes into the butchers shop and James waits outside by the door. She didn't queue or wait to have meat cut, and picks up some pre-packed sausages to take to the counter. CCTV footage shows Denise leaving the shop at 15:39 just two minutes later. She can then be seen running frantically in and out of shot. Also on the CCTV footage is the image of James, in the distance, he is walking with two boys. It is now 15:41 and just four minutes after he arrived outside the butchers.

Once outside the shopping centre James is walked along the busy road. At 15:50 Witness A is on the bus, she sees James from the bus window. She describes in court her horror at seeing him being swung high in the air by his arms as he is walked between the two boys, he is swung so high that she recalls seeing the bottoms of his shoes from the bus window. One of the boys lets go and Witness A lets out a spontaneous shout as James is left dangling, in a painful grip.

No one else on the bus comments. James is also seen by Dry Cleaning delivery man, Witness B who describes the moment James breaks free and runs into the busy road. He is chased and grabbed by one of the boys who brings him back to the footpath. He is also seen by a cab driver and two women pedestrians who all describe similar scenes.

At 16:30 Witness C walks through the subway after collecting her daughter from school. She sees the three boys and one of them is asking another lady for directions to Walton Road Police Station; on getting directions they walk off in the opposite direction. Witness C calls them back. She asks the boys if they are okay and they told her that they had found James in the shopping centre, which was by now one mile away. Witness C asks them why they did not take the boy to the strand police station by the shopping centre. One of them stated that they knew Walton Road Police Station better. One of the boys let go of James' hand and Witness C crouched down to look at him, she held his hand.

In court she describes James as looking tired and

confused. She goes on to tell the court that she felt unable to challenge the two boys further, so she and her daughter continue on home.

At 16:40 Witness D is walking her dog along the canal at Breeze Hill and hears crying coming from the canal tow path. She looked down the bank to see two boys pulling a baby up some steps. In court she recalls the look on James' face he is crying hard and has a large lump on his forehead and another further back.

She describes the moment when she asked the two boys what had happened. She said they replied that the boy had fallen down some steps. She told the two of them to 'hurry him home to his mummy' she added that she thought they were three little brothers.

In court Witness D is cross examined by one of the boys Defending QCs David Turner and he refers Witness D to her original police statement where she had stated 'I asked the two boys if they knew the toddler and they both said they didn't; I told one of the boys that he should get some medical attention for those injuries and they said they would take him to a police station'. Witness D denied the statement in court and denied that she had a duty of care to intervene. Her original signed statement to police had been made 24 hours before James' body was found. Witness D left the boys to continue her dog walk.

Witness E was returning home from near the railway line when he saw three boys in an alleyway. James is described as 'sobbing uncontrollably'. On being noticed by Witness E one of the boys said "I'm sick of minding my little brother after school everyday, I'm gonna tell my mum I don't want to do it any more". The alleyway was dark, it was 17:20 on a cold February evening. The alleyway was near to a shop and the boys were seen by at least three other people who entered the shop. In court Witness E describes knowing the second boy. He was friends with the boy's mother; whom he describes in court as a close friend. He continued on home. He was the fifteenth person and the last adult to see James alive.

Some time after 17:20 James was taken up onto the railway lines, he had blue modelling paint thrown in his face and was beaten to death with bricks. His body then placed on the railway lines.

In their original defence the boys denied abducting James stating that he was lost and had simply followed them. However, in a separate incident some time between lunchtime and 15:40 the two boys had attempted to abduct another two year old boy from the shopping centre but this attempt was foiled by the child's parent who was watching nearby. They were seen on CCTV talking to the two year old and beckoning him to follow them.

Fifteen people saw James after he was taken from the shopping centre that day, many more people witnessed the anti-social behaviour and other attempted abduction that day. If you had been there, if you had been one of those fifteen people;

What would you have done?

The concept of the Bystander Effect is one explanation for the lack of intervention by the public in this case. This concept needs to be understood in order to be able to truly calculate risk. The Phenomena, which has been replicated numerous times, in various studies, works like this; The higher the number of bystanders to an event, the less likely they are to intervene. And this is true regardless of the level of intervention required. These elaborate experiments ranged from observing the bystanders behaviour to a collapsed member of the public, to someone dropping their car keys, to see how many bystanders would help by either picking them up, or alerting the individual.

The phenomena is so strong, that when a waiting room was staged to fill with smoke those waiting, as a group, were more likely to remain seated without raising the alarm. When the waiting room was only occupied by one person, they did in fact act to raise the alarm. The phenomena has demonstrated time and time again that the level of help offered by the passers-by deteriorates, when the number of bystanders increases. The level of deterioration is also sizeable; in the case of the collapsed person, when one bystander was present, they intervened eighty five per cent of the time. When the number of bystanders increased to more than five people, the percentage of those willing to intervene dropped to just thirty percent.

Now, recall the hundred families asked if they would intervene, and consider the findings, that one hundred percent of those who answered, all said they would do something or put simply, they would be physically moved towards either, getting help or getting involved. With none of them opting to walk away.

Studies into the phenomena came about following the case of Kitty Genovese in 1964. Kitty was murdered in an attack by a complete stranger on returning home from work, and despite the attack being a lengthy assault with a knife, and witnessed by 38 bystanders, she was not afforded any assistance. The phenomena, it suggests, is related to a dilution of responsibility and an inherent unwillingness to stand-out in public. This accompanying dilution of responsibility has to teach us that we cannot rely on the kindness of others, we cannot expect the public to intervene, and that if we experience the kindness of strangers and a sense of community where we live; that it is the exception, rather than the rule. Today's society dictates that even when we see something that we know is not right, we may knowingly or unknowingly, chose to do nothing.

It is true that there are random acts of kindness, have a go heroes and those prepared to assist someone in need; we read about them all the time, and see them on the news. But that is because they are newsworthy, outstanding, and rare. If one of those fifteen adults had alerted the police to what they saw that day, bearing in mind that the police were already looking for a missing two year old, then things may have been very different, for James, but, unfortunately - we will never know.

However, what we must know, is what we would do in the same situation.

We have to know how we should, could and would react, when presented with the same scenario. Would we keep it to ourself or would we make the effort to do something? This is why the critical thinking process is so important to protecting our children.

Chapter Seven

Modern Times; Communication & Online Danger

Modern Times: Communication & Online Danger

Communication and online safety go hand in hand and the way that young people communicate is evolving at a terrifying pace. In this digital age, texts, instant chat rooms, selfie's, status' and instagram all roll off the tongue of anyone aged eight to eighteen. But within this new era of communicating, something very important has been lost; the ability to read another person's intentions from their non-verbal cues. This is an essential part of communication and fundamental to any successful communication interaction. When we talk about communication we mean communication as a whole, and this is known as total communication.

Total communication includes the addition of sound, speed of delivery, tonality, volume, visual cues, pauses, body language and the accompanying behaviours. None of which is very conducive to a text message or status. Then there is punctuation, the humble comma and the semi colon are good examples, these are depicted perfectly in Lynne Truss' Eats, Shoots & Leaves;

A woman, without her man, is nothing
Or
A woman: without her, man is nothing.

Nowadays if I send a message to confirm a meeting with a friend, the reply I receive could look something like this;

OK GR8 B@TM CWUL

Then you might ring the person to find out exactly

what they mean, and what they are actually saying is okay, great, busy at the moment, chat with you later! Ah Ha...

At least they didn't reply; H8 U NGTBC (Hate you, not going to bother coming).

But on a serious note, loss of our communication helpers in the form of commas and loss of non-verbal communication is detrimental to our safety. It is a common feature in our ability to calculate risks and make good judgements about another person. When we consider that 93 per cent of communication is non-verbal, then we can begin to equate just how big, a skill erosion is occurring in modern communication.

As parents, we imagine the biggest risk to our children, online, is that of being groomed by a pervert posing as a child in an internet chat room, but this is the thin end of the wedge and so much more is actually going on. Using the internet to communicate is now the preferred method for the majority of UK children and adolescents. So what are some of the dangers and what is being done about it?

The most recent survey conducted by ComRes found that up to 1.5 million people had stumbled upon child abuse images whilst searching the internet. The latest figures surrounding the distribution of indecent child images on the internet is up by 40 percent on last year. The average age of those viewing indecent images of children are in fact children, 88 percent of victims stumbling on child sexual abuse images are children aged ten years or under. More worryingly, 61 percent of these images depicted children being abused by adults, including images of young children being forced to perform sexual acts on adults. Sexual torture and the rape of children by an adult, are also a common theme. Some of the online trend is to encourage children to use their web-cams, now installed on all laptops, these sites offer children counselling about friendship issues or the chance to learn a skill and then some way into the interaction the person indecently exposes themselves to the child.

Equally worrying, is the release of new figures relating to the number of children who regularly have online contact with someone they have never met face to face. This is currently estimated to be 29 percent of UK children aged nine to sixteen. These figures relate to regular visits to websites and chat rooms where the child has regular contact with the same, unknown individual. It is often a requirement of these sites to ask for an email address. Once a child has given an email address a message might be sent asking them to link with their Facebook page and then it isn't very difficult for an individual to find out where your child lives or what school they attend. The introduction of smart phones means that children who update their status by regularly adding places, pictures and people along the way, can then form a social circle that is easily accessible to many. Geo-Tagging or the sharing of geographical identification can be done on any GPS device, smartphone or games console. Even if they were not intending to give out their location they may be doing so by using walk about WiFi with their phones location feature switched on.

In a 2010 survey, 'The Secret Lives of Teens' it was estimated that 65 percent of thirteen to seventeen year-olds regularly included their physical location when communicating. With business and commerce struggling more and more on the high street, it is no surprise that tracking customers and text-offering them discounts when they are within shopping range is becoming the norm. But in order to do this mobile phones and tablet devices have to have the default setting switched on and it is now increasingly more difficult to move around without being digitally visible. The use of portable phones as a valuable lifeline when someone is in danger can now be considered, in part, to contribute to the problem. Not only do we leave a digital footprint of what we do online but also an actual footprint of where we were when we did it.

Online safety is also made more difficult by the ever increasing market in available Apps. Regulation of the App providers is somewhat of a free for all. Apps generated on the foreign market with little regulation are available free to download.

They can be the equivalent of a 'Trojan Horse.' There is little control over the personal information that these Apps can glean from your child's phone and some even install a programme to corrupt the phone. This allows the App producer to access all the data from the phone and has included making calls without the owners knowledge. With 41 percent of twelve to fifteen year-olds owning a smartphone and many more having access to one, regulation of available App's is certainly an ever pressing requirement. There is also an increasing number of *'Phishing'* Apps these target younger users by copying and pasting the home page of one of their more familiar sites and then requesting personal information. Online games for children will often require an adult to add a credit card number for the initial subscription and these *'Phishing'* sites are becoming ever more sophisticated.

Online Sexualisation

The recent concerns over the sexualisation of children draws many links with an overwhelming need to process this instant information and the forming of characteristics in the child that can be described as sexually adult stereotypes.

Children as young as nine are learning that rewards and attention are based on their ability to be desirable to others. Before they are able to process the information it is already forming and shaping their sexual development. The constant obsession with body image is having a negative affect on young children .. some as young as eight years old are presenting in primary health care with initially low mood, low self esteem and later body image issues and depression. It is quite disturbing that girls as young as six years old are fashionably wearing pink tracksuits with 'Booty' emblazoned across their backsides. In a written interview with one sexual predator, he stated that his eight year old victim was 'begging for it' when remarking on how his victim was provocatively dressed. Child Sexualisation has a working definition and can be put simply as; *'The imposing of adult sexuality on to a child or young person before they are capable of dealing with it mentally, emotionally or physically.'*

Understanding Teenage Online Behaviour

One of the problems about promoting online safety to children is that the sites are not very cool. Children are not accessing this information and may not be aware of the risks. There is still no method of evaluating which messages are actually getting through to their intended user.

Communicating online in the teenage world is very different from that of the online adult world and a distinction needs to drawn. Children have a real need to communicate online if they are to be accepted socially within their peer group and the behaviours associated with online communication are dynamically different.

Teenagers gain recognition, support, popularity and

earn their respect from communicating in this arena. The social media-must generation play out their lives in public with the support and 'likes' of their peers. Exchanges can be heated and inflammatory and then resolve as quickly as they started. From a parental point of view, it can be difficult to know when to intervene and being invited to be involved by your child is a real eye opener. Often what is said online would be wholly unacceptable in a face to face exchange. These exchanges are referred to as 'Drama' and involve name calling, shaming, relationship revenges, posting inappropriate pictures with a call to 'comment on' from the peer group and they can play out for a short time or rumble on for days. Interestingly these 'Dramas' attract an audience that choose to watch the unfolding events and either get involved by posting comments or choosing to do nothing – creating a 'virtual bystander' effect.

These dramas, whilst a form of bullying, are not referred to as bullying by the teenagers themselves. Although we see these dramas causing the same low self-esteem issues as bullying, it is evident that for the majority, social networks remain 'a must seen-to-be in place'.

When the Virtual & Real World Collides

The risks for all social net-workers are those dramas that spill over into the real world. There has been for sometime a correlation between the viewing of sexually explicit images and sexual crimes. Both the murderer's of Tia Sharp and April Jones in 2012, had collated enormous libraries of sexual content and in both cases both murderers were first time offenders. It is now considered not beyond reasonable doubt that what a person views in terms of online sexual content will go on to change their behaviour. A move away from using the term child pornography and the recognition, that all sexual images of children are against international law has created a whole new virtual platform to be policed and there just aren't enough resources to cope.

With the circulation of sexually explicit images rising by 40 percent in a year, comes the task of enforcing the law. However, in 2012, the actual prosecution figures were appallingly low. A heated Parliamentary debate in June of this year highlighted the scale of the problem faced by the police force with an admission that they were aware of, and had intelligence on, 60,000 people who swap or download indecent images through established websites, but that they lack the resources to arrest them. When pressed to how many convictions they had obtained on these known assailants the figures were very low indeed. Just 1,570 convictions were obtained. When asking what Ministers intended to do? The Rt Hon Member for Taunton Deane stated;

"There is no point huffing and puffing about the problem, if Ministers do not take the necessary action. It is obvious to the whole country that the current situation is totally unacceptable. It is obvious that Ministers have not got a grip. It is obvious that we need a change"

With popularity being the only currency that our teens now deal in, is it any wonder that we are experiencing the biggest generation gap to date? If Government fail to implement their findings year on year is it any surprise at all that children and their parents are just not listening? When will we see some action on what we need rather than a retrospective, regurgitated account of what we don't need?

Chapter Eight

Social Networks: The Machiavellian Muse

Social Networks: The Machiavellian Muse

Put simply, to be Machiavellian is to be 'someone who schemes in such a way' and often refers to someone who might otherwise be called a bully. It is interesting that at least 9 percent of children using social networking sites claim to have been bullied online. This figure doesn't sound very high until we revisit the fact that teenagers will refer to bullying online as 'Drama' and that to refer to it as bullying would indicate that it is far more extreme. Research by Pew Internet suggests that online behaviour is very different from the behaviour displayed in real life, and warns that your child may not of bullied anyone in real life but may be acting very differently in the digital world.

In reality online bullies display many of the characteristics of real life bullies and as online behaviour becomes the teenagers normal world then we need to ask the question what effect will this have on our children socially? When we know that in order to survive in this harsh arena, teenagers need to be somewhat morally disengaged.

Moral disengagement is the process that enables an individual to convince themselves that bad behaviour is morally acceptable. Teenagers demonstrate these behaviours online by disengaging their moral compass and this can take many forms. It is more easily achievable by dehumanizing victims, a common online communication tactic.

Where has all the Compassion Gone?

Bullies despite being confident, socially successful

and competent are in fact highly deficient in moral compassion when tested for their empathy. This empathetic testing looked at the bullies reactions in comparison to others and in all cases the bullies scored much lower.

In some studies, the ability of bullies to disregard the rights and feelings of others have been compared with similar characteristics displayed by those diagnosed with anti-social personality disorder. Researchers have also drawn correlation between the bullies and their unusual fixed attitudes and beliefs about violence, cruelty and human nature.

Bullies are generally egocentric, providing a rationale for their actions will usually be described in more positive outcomes for themselves. An example might be to describe the attention that they received whilst displaying a total disregard towards their victim in empathetic terms. Any latent moral jitters can often be silenced by passing the incident off as a joke and therefore diluting any feelings of guilt.

When researching bullies Gianluca Gini (2011) also discovered that there are more than one kind of bully. For the first time he separated bullies by their distinct differences and what effect this had on their ability to disengage. What was once thought of as a trait positive in all bullies looks more likely to be the ability of the ordinary, well adjusted persons to disengage morally, in order to inflict harm.

In other words, anyone placed in this hostile environment can become a bully.

Aggression is thought to be key to an ordinary persons ability to switch off their guilt or shame by using one of several mechanisms. These mechanisms of moral disengagement can be described as the process of :-

Dehumanizing or Blaming the Individual – the 'they deserved it' response.

Displacing/Diffusing Responsibility – the 'someone else made me do it' response.

Labelling – the 'it was a joke' or 'it was just a bit of fun' so what's the harm done?

Comparisons – What I have done is not as bad as what others have done, so that makes it okay.

Much evidence exists between the qualities displayed by both bullies, victims and a new sub group of bully/victims. The latter displaying the highest level of depression amongst the group. This new sub group, that may be an online bully that in reality, is a victim of bullying, is most at risk of developing addiction as well as other personality disorders. In one study there is a correlation for those who have been victimised online, being the most likely to behave inappropriately online into their adulthood. This involved the online viewing of inappropriate images. The link is that over exposure to online sexualisation had caused them to display confusion or disappointment in their own sexuality, as adulthood approached.

Poor habitat and erosion of social roles for young adults is also a contributing factor and the study highlights, this as being the change within a person rather than the simplistic view that this is primarily a genetic or chemical disorder. The poor habitat and loss of role is an area under further study. The loss of social boundaries that accompany this state are also considered causal in an increase in opportunistic offences on victims. In other words, they may not have chosen to go online with the intent to bully someone, but then the opportunity presents itself. Prolonged exposure within this arena, thought to take place at a time when the young mind is forming, is thought to be responsible for the increase in drug and alcohol addiction – in the young.

> *"the long-term effects of childhood sexual victimisation are psychological disorder, with marked risk for the development of alcohol and drug misuse"* (Watkins & Bentovim, 2006)

The report goes further to suggest that anti-social arenas have a marked effect on the brains ability to deal with even mild problems. The exposure to the developing mind may also apply filters, that are typically anti-social. The result is that future interactions in life are then viewed through this filter and will be responsible for a distorted reaction, that is not based in reality or social norm.

> *"Exposure to anti-social models is also likely to teach individuals maladaptive ways of solving personal problems and interpersonal problems and result in problematic values and attitudes, which will have an impact upon the perception and memory system"*
> (Watkins & Bentovim, 2006)

This paints a pretty poor picture for those in 'Social Networks' who are behaving less than socially, fresh minds for forming, but at what cost? Is this just 'Drama' or is it something far more indicative of a future social problem?

Chapter Nine

The Government Responds to Online Safety......Badly

The Government Responds to Online Safety .... Badly

The problem with operating from a reactive stance as opposed to being proactive, when it comes to government, is that it is very difficult to claw back or pass changes in law for what has already gone before.

When we witnessed a public outcry over online gambling and the rise of the super casinos, Government, under pressure from the public, had to act. This led to the implementation of some very robust age verification filters. The pressure applied by the public, generated action, as the public understood the problem and was enabled to react.

Most insulting to parents is the fact that they have been kept in the dark on both the risks of child abduction and to the extent of exposure to indecent images.

Equally frustrating is knowing that the technology exists, certainly from computer manufacturers and Internet Service Providers (ISP) to give us these robust safety filters. In fact in other European countries it is an operational demand. These filters, that Labour put in pace for gambling, are in the public's best interest. But are the public aware of them? Do the public source their computers or install software with filters as the default setting? I suggest many do not, it did not come up in the survey as something that parents would chose to use. As disappointing as this is, we also have to be realistic about the current ability of our parental filters, which really are not up to speed, when compared with our European neighbours.

Without these filters, not only are our younger generation able to access inappropriate content but they are also open to images, Apps, websites and chat-rooms all operated from outside the UK. Children are heavily targeted from outside the UK and without other safety warnings they may not even realise that they have passed through a global gateway. Splash Warning pages are a second recommendation already available and yes they are already in place in other countries. It seems that the UK will not allow a ten year old child to watch a 12a film at the cinema, but they can certainly watch an XX-Rated one in the comfort of their own home.

When I revisit the APCC Update and Meetings Feedback Report accessed in November 2013, I am astonished that following the Independent Parliamentary Inquiry into Online Child Protection, completed in April 2012, we are still no further forward in addressing its very stark warning. The recommendations suggested;

1: The Government should urgently review the implementation plans for 'Active Choice' and press for an accelerated implementation timetable, more clarity on installation targets for all customers, and funding commitments from ISPs.

2: ISPs should provide better support for internet safety education and initiatives such as ParentPort and improve signposting for these services from their own web domains.

3: Government and industry representatives should draw up guidelines for improving the communication of existing internet safety settings, improving training for retailers, developing a family friendly kite-marking scheme for manufacturers and retailers and improving signposting to pre-installed security settings during device configuration.

4: ISPs should be tasked with rolling out single account network filters for domestic broadband customers that can provide one click filtering for all devices connected to a home internet connection within 12 months.

5: The Government should launch a formal consultation on the introduction of an opt-In content filtering system for all internet accounts in the UK. The most effective way to reduce overall development cost and create the most flexible solution would be for ISPs to work together to develop a self-regulated solution.

6: Public WiFi provision should also be filtered in this way otherwise home-based controls will be easily circumvented.

7: The Government should also seek backstop legal powers to intervene should the ISPs fail to implement an appropriate solution.

8: Finally, the Government should consider the merits of a new regulatory structure for online content, with one regulator given a lead role in the oversight and monitoring of internet content and in improving the dissemination of existing internet safety education materials and resources such as ParentPort.

This Inquiry, was independent and despite this the panel was made up of seventeen MPs with involvement from a total of sixty more MPs contributing; "How many MPs does it take to change a policy?" Answer: clearly more than sixty, because nearly two years after the recommendations – I couldn't find much evidence of anything constructive. Although I note that the wider consultation in recommendation (5) was carried out. However, it was a blunder on the part of the Government as they failed to consult correctly and what followed was a grade A cock-up on a grand scale. The consultation was to establish how many, if any parents wanted parental controls switched on as a default setting.

Presumably this sort of consultation would need to consult parents if it was deemed to be taken seriously. But the Government failed to ask parents in any number that could be demonstrable. This led one of the panel; Helen Goodman MP, to speak out, asking the question, indirectly through Ed Vaizey MP,

'Why did the Government not introduce a communications Bill with appropriate measures in the Queens Speech?'

Of those consulted less than 35 percent were parents and the rest were a lobbying group of 1,500 members. The parental group consulted, and representative of Britain's 11 million children, were not heard and the consultation concluded that parents had in fact voted against seeing parental controls set as default. How convenient was that? No action required then.

When a heated debate ensued at the House, a typical, tactical response was retorted by Ed Vaizey MP, who proceeded to list all of the Conservative Party's past achievements. The response began with reiterating, in 1,000 odd words, how appalling he thought Online Child Exploitation was, well done Ed....good diesel smoking answer to cover up your Governmental shortcomings.

So when can we expect what 78 percent of parents want, in a separate YouGov poll, this was information for the government and not carried out by them, clearly. Well, at the current rate of progress the estimate is 2019. So what advice has the Government been disseminating in the meantime? What has the Government done with the research data from

University College London, that suggests Splash Pages reduce the viewing of inappropriate content by at least Half? discovered in their research and offered up to Government. The answer to both questions is nothing, in case you were wondering.

Looking at this inaction just begs the question; what's really going on? Why is nothing being done? Who is in bed with who here? It is interesting to note that many of the ISPs, most mobile phone companies and other dubious collaborations are all 'Partner Members' to the CEOP. Paying money to Government Departments to attend meetings, make promises and then sell the recommended products such as filters, as an additional cost to parents. Call me a sceptic, but I did not receive any leaflets on child safety or filters, in my son's new mobile phone packaging, bought from a high street store of one of the 'Partners' so what exactly are they all doing at their three monthly meetings, with lunch laid on?

Meanwhile, back at the House, A now frustrated Jeremy Browne MP is about to have his say and the Rt Hon Member holds no punches, when he states:

"So what have the Government been doing? Before the general election, the Prime Minister promised that he would lead the most family-friendly Government ever, but so far there has been lots of talking and much less action. After three years and two Secretaries of State, the Government still seem to think that a voluntary approach will work. Do they not know when they are being strung along, or do they not care? How many more years must we wait? How many child deaths will it take to shock them into action?

Two years prior to this, the Government failed again to adhere to its own announced deadline for ISPs and others in the internet industry.

> *"they must, as a matter of urgency, act decisively to develop and introduce effective parental controls – with Government regulation if voluntary action is not forthcoming within a reasonable time scale – and robust age verification."*

Presumably this was before they were invited to partner with the CEOP and our now 'National Crime Agency.'

What we do know is that of the 60,000 individuals and websites swapping indecent images of children, just 1,570 convictions have taken place. There is very little data to support the fact but I suspect that many of these sites are not UK based and that may be the problem with the low conviction rate. The problem of these sites would certainly be wiped out by a robust age verification filter or at the very least their demand would be cut by the use of Splash-Warning Pages.

If we look to the hailed pioneers of internet safety – namely the Internet Watch Foundation (IWF) we can see that they too have a list of 'partners' many of these partners are the same organisations holding a seat at the CEOP. And what of their work? Of the 1.5million people stumbling on indecent child images last year just 40,000 were reported to the IWF Hotline and the IWF, like the CEOP, admit being overwhelmed with the task – sounds like the perfect time for that filter then, doesn't it?

Chapter Ten

Appeasing the Public with Public Inquiries

Appeasing the Public with Public Inquiries

What's in it for us? Public Inquiries are something similar to a knee jerk reaction. Lengthy, and on completion, they are jargon filled, cumbersome, documents, that are not for public consumption.

To a sceptic, they are an expensive remedy to a public outcry. They go on to inform Government and their recommendations are the by-products of in-depth enquiry. For the record they are headed up by leaders in their field, the best possible are sourced. Without hesitation those chosen are the 'no stone unturned' variety, top drawer, best in the industry – specialists. But what ever comes of all their hard work – their findings? and What's in it for us?

Of the many recommendations evidenced in these reports, that sometimes take two years to produce. What actually happens, changes, or gets implemented?

How many Victoria Climbie's, Baby P's, and Daniel Pelka's do we need to endure before we, as parents say, hang on a minute – haven't we heard this before?

If X-Factor gave us the same winner, singing the same song, two years in a row then the news papers would be reporting on an angry mob all demanding that heads should roll. We can be aggressive when X-Factor get it wrong, but when these public inquiries come out of public funds and achieve very little, we do nothing about it, zero, zilch, not even a murmur from us, as the Government plunges its metaphorical hand deep into our pockets. The recommendations in these reports, stay in these reports and nobody demands an explanation as to why they have not been implemented. Well, keep your ear to the ground and keep your eyes open, the next child abduction is coming. The next child to be starved, beaten and invisible to the authorities is out there. I can predict that before I have finished writing this book, another child will be killed or grotesquely abused in some way, and that's not because I'm psychic or a witch. It has simply become a case of mathematics – the risk determines the number, we currently have no control over it.

What then?, what's in it for us? A slow and painful daily saturation of the facts, via the media, on what neighbours saw, and teachers who suspected but did nothing, healthcare professionals who examined but failed to notice, and social workers who called to see but only left a card. With every case, weeks or months will pass and we will be drip fed the story of either, a monster-parent, her torturous lover and their unmonitored conduct, despite being on a register to do just that, or a mental patient or released, protected-paedophile. That they are now unequivocally sorry about, whilst they scapegoat someone else. That gets the fired only to appeal and be re-hired after a hefty fat-cat compensation for their despair, aren't we just sick of it? Well, we are not the only ones.

The experts compiling these inquiries are asking questions too. If these reports are to restore the public's confidence in these services, then they have failed. If these inquiries are announced, to restore public confidence in the Government then they have failed. The real question has to be who ever benefits from the information and findings? One could suggest that they are safeguards that might stop to a similar case happening, But we cannot, realistically make that claim either.

When a Serial abductor with a string of sixteen convictions, for rape, attempted rape and violence against young girls, was given a job in a school. We had to ask ourselves, how was it possible? Lord Bichard was then tasked with the role of heading the Inquiry. It was the murder of the two bright young girls by their school caretaker, whom should never have secured the post in the first place, that was under review. The Bichard Inquiry was to provide us with the answers.

In a catalogue for errors – Ian Huntley's file of 16 plus inquiries and cautions was deleted By Humberside Police due to their unknown right to retain it or pass the information on to the Police National Computer – Database. They simply deleted it, so as not to infringe the serial rapists human rights. When Huntey then applied for the role at the School, the Criminal Records Bureau was for him, the same minor irritation that it is for all working professionals, when it came back clear within six weeks.

It was the Bichard Inquiry that highlighted the catastrophic communication failings between neighbouring police forces with different computer systems, who in turn did not collaborate or work inter-professionally to share this information either amongst themselves or the Police National Computer. Can we, several years later say unreservedly, that this could never happen again? Unfortunately we cannot.

Bringing the computer systems of the various UK police forces up to speed and recording their data in an accurate and timely manner is still not a reality. The mechanisms to share such data too has been described as ' only as good as the person inputting that data'.

In June this year, we will be ten years post Bichard.

So what have we achieved, if anything, for our £10 million public spend? The employment and safety procedures in schools have certainly tightened and the CRB checks system have been revamped. But from the list of recommendations passed to Government, not a great many have been implemented. The author himself describes the lack of use of his findings as "deeply depressing" So distraught is the author of the report and its quoted 'entirely reasonable findings' that he took to lobbying Government Ministers himself. The actions of Lord Bichard were justified when he gave his contribution to the Gresham College Debate. He cites any progress on the Police National Database as being a result of his lobbying behind the scenes to Senior Ministers outside of the reports recommendations. He describes a "remarkable reluctance to learn and adapt to the changes identified by these enquiries, in so many professions".

Lady Justice Janice Smith, responsible for chairing the enquiry into Harold Shipman echoed these comments. The Shipman Inquiry's costs stand at £21million pounds of public money. Lady Smith concluded that "looking at enquiries as a whole, are they worth the time and money and resources? I would like to say yes but it's often a close run thing". Not such a close run thing when the comparison is drawn between the 'Bloody Sunday and 9/11 Inquiries. Leverson, the report is a 5,000 page document that has taken twelve years to complete. The cost to the UK is said to be £195million, and none of this is compensation for the families. By contrast, The 9/11 report is 2.5million pages taking twenty months to complete and the cost was only $15million US Dollars. Someone has gotten rich off of our funds yet again.

Although this has been labelled as a disaster by our

own Prime Minister, it is just another example of the Government's ability to find what money they deem necessary, at the expense of other people's lives. The legal expenses which are ludicrous figures appearing to be plucked from the sky have been published and anyone who has lost a son or daughter, whilst fighting for this country and its Government in the last twelve years; might be interested to note that The Ministry of Defences bill for legal costs, for Leverson, ran to £32,553,738. And for any of those families about to send their children to war, you can be advised that they will not be getting any 'much needed' protective equipment soon. But you can rest assured, the fourteen other lawyers that made up the legal teams and earned in excess of 4million pounds each, will be watching them die on their Plasma Screens, along with our abducted and murdered children, for which they will not be unequivocally sorry, I'm sure.

This Government's practice of being reactive, albeit under public pressure, rather than proactive is destroying much needed public funds, that would otherwise be destined for families, hospitals, and education. The reaction to the publishing of the costs involved in inquiries is also something our own Prime Minister 'reacted' to by stating in parliament *"let me reassure the House that there will be no more open-ended and costly inquiries into the past."*

Presumably that will be after the conclusions of Operation Ore and Jimmy Saville, which could eclipse the Bloody Sunday Inquiry, in terms or pages. Not to mention Operation Fairbank and Fernbridge, and the nineteen plus hospitals carrying out their own Inquiries from their own diverted funds. What we will then need is an enquiry into our inquiries and the loss of public funds that simply might of ring-fenced or secured some funding to form a definition of UK Child Abduction.

Another one of our MPs had something to say about this too. Justice Secretary, Ken Clarke, (*yes, that man*) told Leverson " The Media now has more power than Parliament and have the capacity to drive a weak government like a flock of sheep before them" 'Well, lets hope it's over a cliff, but unlike Robin Cook, because that was just yet another cover up', according to Barrister Michael Shrimpton. And we will have to wait for another Public Inquiry or scoping report into that too. Ken Clarke also commented on the life of parliamentarians in days gone by, when he stated "Everybody in politics, even a minor parliamentary candidate, knew that the then Prime Ministers wife had been having a torrid affair with a backbencher for at least 30 previous years. Not a word of this ever appeared in public print" '*Oh those really were the good old days, weren't they Ken*', he continued "currently a Prime Minister would last two or three days if an affair became public knowledge". Here, here.....lets hope the same applies to you too.

Really, appeasing the public and trying to keep a lid on this, this bin full of rotting 'pounds of flesh' must be a parliamentary nightmare for poor Ken. One question I couldn't get answered was how much of the parliamentary expenses (Scandal) was actually money spent on paedophile pick-ups, to and from Dolphin Square, London. Perhaps it was recorded as a petrol or leisure expense, since it involved the use of a parliamentary Jag and was someone's idea of leisure.

Chapter Eleven

The Human Cost of Trafficking

The Human Cost of Trafficking

The reason that Child Abduction is such a Hot-Topic and the rationale for applying pressure for a clear cut definition is simply, this child abduction is an act that precedes more than one type of crime. The notion that an opportunist creeps up and swipes a child, is a myth. It happens, but it is a rarity. The greater threat to our children is the risk of abduction to order. Not only is abduction seen to be an act that satisfies an individuals warped sense of need, but also that our children are now a commercial entity. Take that in for a moment....your child is worth money and a lot of money is changing hands. The industry has an estimated turnover of $32 Billion Dollars and an estimated 21 million victims, globally.

When these gangs go shopping for children, they don't hang around in parks or carry thirsty puppies, who need your child's help. They are sophisticated, stealth- like and their activity is on the rise. It is this type of abductor who is thought to be responsible for taking Madeline McCann. A child, stolen to order. They are difficult to track down, their movements are global, as are their customers. Customers wanting your children as slaves, child soldiers, for illegal adoption and as sex slaves.

Child Pornography – as it is referred by its industry has 'pay days' that rival the Hollywood Film Industry and they are big with a capital B. Their films, about the worst type of imagery that you can dare to imagine, changes hands for up to £5,000 a copy. Often sold as limited editions that raise the prices through the roof and for a very hefty fee can be viewed in the making – a snuff-movie on-set-view was sold to a man in an Amsterdam Café, meet and greet, for £45,000. He of course declined.

With the recent close, in October 2013, of the first Online Global Conference – hailed as a great success in bringing together expert speakers and child victims.

Together, we can begin to get an idea of the bigger picture. The three day event, we can hope, will be repeated next year with an even greater collaboration of those in the industry. UNICEF estimate that 2 million children are trafficked every year – their destination is the sex trade and that for every three children trafficked globally, two are girls and one is a boy. It further warns that behind everyone of these statistics is a real child.

So, how exactly are they taking our children? UNICEF also suggest that 76 percent of transactions for sex with under-age girls starts on the internet. But how?

For younger children there is the known risk of families on holiday. Young children, in popular resorts are easier to separate from their parents on a much needed wind-down. Many socially unacceptable norms are lessened on a well earned break. And these parents are not being kept informed of the risks, for the obvious reasons, damage to the resorts global trade. Rich and inconspicuous people fit well into these environments and they are buying information from holiday *transient* workers.

Information on where you are staying and the ages of your children are currency to the poorly paid and seasonal hired help.

Equally, just because you have paid a lot for your annual getaway, it doesn't mean that the hotel staff or beach workers are not selling your details to a well paying gang. The rigour of checks on holiday workers outside the UK, is not a safeguard and this transient population of workers are free to move about working both freelance and on daily rates. For older children we need to be aware that the internet is their biggest risk. But before you go and tear up your tickets for a week in the sun and head off to center parcs and its protective dome, remember we are talking about a global risk.

Facebook has an estimated 80 million fake accounts. Naked Security ran a piece about this and asked bloggers to comment on their experiences. What was interesting about the bloggs was that many people were able to articulate exactly what effect this had on their use of the social network. So who are these fakers?

Facebook has 955 Million users

Facebook has 45 Million duplicate account holders,

Facebook has 23 Million accounts assigned to pets, businesses and other.

Facebook has 14 Million accounts dedicated to malicious activity.

Despite being a violation of Facebook's Terms & Conditions these bogus accounts remain in activity. When questioned about the accounts Facebook suggest that the problem in the UK is a small part of the problem and the real problems stem from the emerging markets such as Indonesia and Turkey. But this is Facebook right? There are no global gateways.

So before your twelve year announces to the whole world that you will be going to one of these emerging markets for your annual jolly's – think again.

As much as Facebook is a part of our everyday lives we have to be aware that there are many unhappy facebookers out there – one blogger referring to it as Fraudbook after receiving a barrage of unwanted contacts for a business link he posted. Another claiming that he was unable to shut an account down because of the bogus friends he had failed to 'like' prevented him from doing so.

"Fancy a low fat Bagel? How about a Virtual Bagel? When BBC Technology Correspondent Rory Cellan-Jones set up London Based Virtual Bagel Ltd, he got 1,600 likes for his Virtual Bagels within 24 hours. The Facebook page had no interesting content but offered to send its customers a digital form of numerical zeros as 'Virtual Bagels'. Funny as this was nearly all the 'likes' came from India, Egypt, Indonesia and the Philippines. The BBC reporter also stated that the page was most liked by 13 to17 year-olds in Cairo, on contacting the lucky recipients of the Virtual Bagels these account holders were found not to be children at all.

Facebook later claimed that it had an automated system in place to track fake account holders. I suspect that the fake account holders have been known to Facebook for some time. But, with a stock market flotation looming, having 955 million users would have helped rack up the over priced deal, estimated to be 30 Billion Dollars overpriced when valued by Morgan Stanley and Nasdaq Exchange.

Facebook is just one of the social networking sites tasked with providing security to its users and there are many more players emerging in this lucrative market. Snapchat, Instagram to name a further two. Human Trafficking needs a vehicle to operate and social media sites are easy to set up. It is a sad fact that many adults are making a lucrative living online by posing as a child, a likeable actor or film star. There are currently numerous Ronaldo's out there and Beckham's ready to give young users another piece of the wisdom that made them famous.

Every child, it seems, wants to be famous these

days, and they are prepared to risk it all in a bid to be in with a chance. I know it, you know it and the organised gangs online know it too.

Chapter Twelve

Global Indecency

Global Indecency

The US Communications and Decency Act 1996 was set up to prevent minors from viewing indecent images on the Net. Husband and wife team, Thomas and Janice Reedy decided that they would do something about it. In response to the 1996 Act, they set up Landslide, an age verification portal. Internet surfers would need to go through this portal in order to access adult content sites. By paying the Reedy's a monthly subscription of approx $29.00 US Dollars surfers would gain access to images and sites that might otherwise take a lifetime to find by themselves.

Remember that there is nothing illegal with adults paying for adult content pornography to view on their own equipment if they are not intending to distribute it and it is for their own personal use. The Texan based couple were clearly on to something and the service they provided racked up a massive ten million US dollars in a two year period. Within this time the site continued to evolve and this point is key to the investigation. In a bid to maximise their profit margin the Reedy's began selling advertising space on the Landslide site. This was at a time when 'pop-ups and Banners' were starting to become common place in high traffic sites. A common feature of all these types of advertising are the point of sale or 'call to action' often displayed as a 'click here' function. These are still commonplace on today's portals and some are highly aggressive to be noticeable. Some even have the ability to trace or predict your mouse movements and move around the screen so that you click on them without really intending to.

As the Reedy's project evolved further, they saw the financial gain in adding additional services to a site that was by now gaining additional daily memberships.

One of the services to be added to the site in 1998, was Keyz - a secondary portal or gateway. Keyz was unlike any service that had been available before.

Part of the problem of children viewing adult content, in the US, was the ever growing need for users of these sites to distribute images amongst themselves.

Sent unsecured, these images were finding their way onto the mainstream Net. The problem was that accessing the many sites containing pornography were monthly subscription sites that carried an average six month subscription. So for users on the look out for new images, they were highly expensive. The six monthly subscription required adult verification using credit card details, these were then verified by the sites and this was not instant access. The Reedy's knew that offering an adult verification gateway would allow some of these sites to drop the lengthy subscriptions that they needed in order to verify users and offer them access for instant viewing for a subscription of one week at a time.

A year into the service and Keyz was a secondary portal providing access to over four hundred sites without the cumbersome subscription or repetitive adult verification service to view each image. One credit card subscription to Landslide was a better option to appear on the users credit card statement instead of multiple pay-per-views. The problem with Keyz was that, once through the portal, users had to make choices about the sites they wanted to go to. Advertising Pop-Ups were aggressive and although the majority of Keyz sites were adult pornography, some did however, contain access to child pornography sites.

Viewing the images of child pornography is in fact illegal and is, by it's very nature, 'child abuse' as any child taking part in these 'Child Pornography' images would not be a willing participant and would therefore have suffered harm.

In 1999, the Police in Fort Worth, Texas were preparing to expose, what was later described as, the biggest paedophile ring in existence. The secret raid - 'Operation Avalanche'- was set to change the lives of many unsuspecting individuals on a global scale. The raid secured Landslide's servers and data bases and the Reedy's were released on police bail, pending the results of the databases decoding. The now multiple millionaire husband and wife team quickly reinstated their operation as they firmly believed they were not breaking any laws. They instructed lawyers to argue out their innocence.

The Reedy's downfall was their failure to recognise that although the sites that used their gateway were not their own they were, as owners of the servers, ultimately responsible for the *distribution* of child pornography. The global suppliers of the sites to the gateway simply slipped away and were never pursued. To break the law in Texas is one thing but to be responsible for distributing indecent images of children, in Texas, was to hit hard. Thomas Reedy was sentenced eight months after his servers were seized and his sentence was 15 years for every image that had passed through the portal, to run consecutively. His original sentence was for 1,335 years imprisonment, this was appealed and later reduced to 180 years.

With the Reedy's now out of business the Texan Police were getting closer to decoding the server files and when they had finished they had in their possession the contact and credit card details of the 390,000 memberships to Landslide. Of this figure only 35,000 turned out to be US credit card holders; the rest were global memberships. The Police found 26,462 UK transactions that had passed through the Landslide portal and these related to 7,272 credit card holders in the UK. The problem with the Landslide memberships and transactions were that they were all recorded together, in one server. Those who had paid for access to *legal* adult sites and those that had clicked to enter child pornography images. The US police set about distributing the data they had collected to the various countries involved with their accompanying advice, based on their own intelligence which was ongoing. The advice was, to the receiving authorities, treat each individual as a potential child abuser.

This police intelligence was based on the covert data gathered prior to the raid. The Dallas Detective in charge of the operation used Web Buddy 'catch-alls' attached to twelve different and falsified memberships. The data captured from each site was stored in the buddy system and formed the evidence that child pornography was being accessed. The problem with this evidence was that it may have captured access to the original Landslide gateway and further traffic through to the Keyz portal but it did not separate Keyz requests for adult content over request to re-direct the user to child pornography sites. It captured frames and images, some had adverts or Pop-Ups offering child pornography but they did not prove adequately, that they had, indeed, been accessed. There has been talk of the images that were re-traced through the internet archives, and then used as evidence, as being cropped or digitally altered in some way.

This data would go on to form 'Operation Ore'

The high profile nature of Operation Ore, that was launched with the help of the BBC in May 2002, has been an enormous financial drain both in terms of the costs to our police service and to those who lives were destroyed, by being falsely accused of accessing child pornography. The pressure on the police to deliver the hastily announced 7,272 UK individuals has led to the use of different tactics within different police forces. Some suspects were sent messages stating 'we know what you are doing – stop it' or 'we are coming for you'. To date this has led to some thirty three suicides with suspects in high profile careers and further arrests including 250 Police Officers, General Practitioners, Military, Teachers and Our Politicians.

In 2005, The Guardian reported on the case of Commander Tom Herman the 48 year old Naval Officer and Queens former Harbour Master; who had been charged on counts of deliberately downloading indecent images of underage children. The charges were dropped and he was cleared with the warning that the prosecution should never have come to this. The twelve images found to have been downloaded by Herman were girls in Bikinis and represented what Mr Woollard, Portsmouth Magistrate said, were the tamest images he had ever seen used as prosecution evidence. Mr Herman's fantasies and curiosity had not involved any pay-per-view material.

In a separate case some four months before British Navel Commodore David White and a commander of Gibraltar based British Forces was not so lucky. After being informed that he was an Operation Ore suspect, the 51 year old took his own life. Hundreds more suspects are awaiting their fate and it is this process of waiting that has caused such trauma. Commander White was found dead in his swimming pool, alone, and there has still been no evidence to suggest that he accessed child pornography images from the Landslide Portal.

The investigation that has cost Britain Millions is ongoing with more than 900 cases close to pre-arrest and a further 1,400 arrested, bailed and pending decoding of their home computers. Many give accounts of having their lives disrupted at best and destroyed at worst. In some cases children have been removed from their home and placed on the 'At Risk Register' there are broken marriages and lost employment and homes, in a process that is now being brought into question based on the production and admission of the altered evidence. Whilst the cases are appealed and argued out in a case by case, lengthy process then the treatment of a further 500 suspects were given poor to non existent advice and settled for a caution that they believed would end in a non-custodial or criminal record outcome.

Now realising that this immediately added them to the Sex Offenders Register for five years.

The numbers now appearing on the register are disproportionately showing a raise and of the 3,700 arrested so far, this has resulted in 109 cases where children within these families who were considered at risk, have been removed from their homes. Some of the suspects warrant this treatment but there seems to be little, if any, robust evidence. And when detectives from Dallas, were brought in to verify their testimonies, there was an admissions of evidence tampering that will now call into question all of the suspects both pending and proven cases. There is, however, no doubt that the pressure piled on Commander David White, a man educated at Eton, with an exemplary career record, was too much to bear and ultimately caused him to end his own life.

The fall out continues along with the spiralling costs and if we have questions about Operation Ore we should be looking to those responsible to at least estimate the costs, the length of time it will take and the contributions from the much needed public purse. One case alone is estimated to be in the region of £750,000 in costs to a falsely accused business man from Watford. The Man who will not be named has had to wait eight years to have his name cleared. The case was without evidence and cost the UK business man his livelihood and put a strain on his marriage. What is important here is the Police Forces free reign to continue spending money from the public purse in pursuing a case that they were advised by their own computer experts, to have no evidence of any access to indecent images.

The man in question had his credit card fraudulently used on the Landslide website, he had contacted Landslide at the time and was given a full refund. The police did find indecent images from the Landslide Website. They were found on one of his business computers, and to answer the question of how they may have got there in the first place, left the police computer forensics expert with the task of explaining. The reason that these indecent images appeared on his computer were quite astounding. These images were adverts or thumbnails, that were sent to his email account. After the man emailed the Texan site to complain about the fraudulent use of his credit card, the Landslide server began an email advertising campaign, by return. There was a clear timeline of events and the police were advised of this. The fact that this man was receiving images delivered to his computer due to his original contact and that these images, although not viewed, were now stored in his computer hard drive were now seen as evidence enough to rack up a 750k prosecution bill. My point is that we are all open to this type of scam and so could equally have our lives destroyed.

Questions

Do we always know what's being accessed on our home computers?

Is our Cyber Safety really as secure as we would like to think?

Haven't we all been plagued by aggressive Pop-Up Advertisements?

If we have accepted cookies, don't we then get target campaigned with similar likes?

Do you now still think it could never happen to you?

And the most important question that needs to be asked is, Who are the professionals in high places, that Operation Ore is failing to Name?

Chapter Thirteen

The VIP's - Very Important Paedophile

VIPs - Very Important Paedophile

Paedophiles aren't monsters. "Steady on, don't shut the book, jump up and down on it, and then kick it around the room, I know what I just said." But it is really important that we all get this. Paedophiles aren't monsters so we can stop looking for them in caves or under large rocks. Generally speaking they do not hang around in dirty coats with bags of sweets. We need to stop pedalling this convenient image NOW. Paedophilia is about power so, you need to consider people in power and people who wantonly demonstrate power. Think suits, cash or positions of privilege.

Positions of unchallengeable access to impressionable young children. Paedophiles who do not demonstrate this are certainly seeking this power over someone else. Secondly, paedophiles in positions of power are usually very successful people, charismatic, likeable and not very obvious. The reason they are not very obvious is generally, they do not believe that what they are doing is wrong.

So they do not need to appear to be different, they don't need a different look or an obvious style that stands out in a crowd. They are not likely to be shrinking violets or oddities with many cats . They believe that what they are doing may not be acceptable, but that it is normal, albeit, to them. The human brain cannot reconcile an act that is performed countless times, whilst remaining unacceptable to the person carrying it out. Otherwise they would need to posses the mind of a psychopath. There are those type of

Paedophiles too. But if paedophiles are successful in all other areas of their life, then they do not carry the belief that there is something wrong with them or their sexuality. It is just important for us all to note this point. They believe that what they get pleasure from is actually normal.

The reason that the link with Parliament is so strong is that before paedophilia was driven underground, it was a very open affair. In the 1980s, paedophiles were seeking to have themselves recognised as a minority group. Many infiltrated the Gay Rights movements of the late seventies in a bid to be recognised in this way.

Many years ago a study was completed, by an MP, into paedophilia and the belief at that time was one of paedophilia being a reciprocal relationship. Why? Well, it was a report conducted by paedophiles, about paedophiles, for the benefit of paedophiles and yes the public funded it.

Children as young as four were thought to display sexual feelings and paedophiles argued to have this recognised. This would seem impossible, even ludicrous to the average person, but it's true. The MP, from his findings, drew up a manifesto on the rights of paedophiles and the rights of young children to be in a reciprocal relationship and display their feelings. This manifesto was given to the then parliamentarian Leon Brittan MP. And in their closed little Government world, it was taken seriously. Luckily the manifesto that called for the age of consent to be lowered to just four years old didn't get heard in the House and no one knows what became of the original report, citing to be the evidence.

There was to be, however, a catastrophic error. The gay rights movement of the mid 1970s, was a rather small affair and it realised that by allowing paedophiles to join their ranks, their numbers would swell. This involved joint or collaboratively focused rallies and national conferences. This led to many paedophiles posing as gay men in order to remain undetected. The reason for wanting to remain undetected was at first puzzling because they didn't believe that they were doing anything wrong, and in their mind the age of consent would soon be lowered, and they would then be legitimatised. The reason for wanting to remain undetected was far more sinister and it was because the gay rights movement had the sympathy of the public and paedophiles just didn't. The public didn't want the age of consent lowered to four years old and were rallying themselves to say so. The spotlight shone more favourably on gay rights at this time.

Then another catastrophic failing occurred, Islington Council was the first to come forward and publicly speak out that it would change it's equal opportunities policy to encompass gay people. A recruitment drive focused solely on appointing gay people within the local authority commenced. Nothing wrong with that at all. But paedophiles now posing as gay men were then welcomed with open arms. This led to a second catastrophic error in allowing paedophiles to head the lead in twelve of the boroughs children's homes. The newly appointed, undercover, gay men wasted no time in closing ranks and employing their own kind. This led to the first organised child pornography network being born, It was systematic, and quickly embedded into the organisations culture. Children were rented out, photographed, abused by the homes staff and it's string of regular, unsavoury visitors. This was cultivated, institutional abuse and those children who were the most vulnerable or did not have parents fighting for their return, were moved around the country in a 'cash for sex' scandal to outside customers of which there were many. When mistakes or injuries occurred the boys were simply killed and nobody asked any questions.

With their positions of power now secure the paedophile network went on to corrupt others in power. Some Judges were frequent customers and a practice to protect their most favoured boys involved making them 'Wards of the Court'.

Nobody asked any questions when these boys disappeared, were sent abroad, or snuffed.

There was an organisation at the time, listening to the boys and trying to access the network. The National Association for Young People In Care, (NAYPIC), Had two social workers at the this time, Mary Moss and Chris Fay. He has given us the names of some of the VIPs involved, and users of the service. He has survived one assassination attempt and he talks about this too. You can view his very interesting interview on Youtube under pie'n'mash films (this is the name of the film company who filmed it).

The Campaign for Homosexual Equality (CHE) continued and gathered pace, this strong movement held regular meets up and down the country and remained accompanied by their paedophiles delegates until the mid eighties, before eventually severing all ties. These meetings openly sold copies of the Manifesto on paedophile rights with its desire to lower the age of consent amongst other things. These meetings were always hotly attended by MPs wanting to show their support.

Entering the mid eighties, the paedophile network was stronger, a second network was established, this was in Lambeth and had been influenced by Islington's 'successful policy', its full quota of staff, and activities were now running high. The Network needed meeting places and facilities in order to function at this level. With the separation from the Gay Rights network came the paedophile information exchange or PIE. Off shoots from PIE included the Paedophile membership only' club Spartacus. The problem arose with its membership and it attracted a global movement of more hardcore and sadistic paedophiles. Boys were being taken on trips to Holland and other destinations in the Spartacus network, some did not return. Their care records, which were private documents under 'wards of the court', were inaccessible and filled large, cumbersome, filing cabinets, that have just simply disappeared.

At the same time, The Gay Rights movement had its own agenda, to protect those working within these high profile positions. They applied pressure to have policies in place that would protect them. One policy on anti harassment meant that it was impossible to have a case heard by the protective boroughs, if it was about the conduct of a gay employee. The paedophiles still working as the boroughs now prized gay employment quota had the protection they needed. Although some people were aware of what was going on and were bringing their cases to the attention of their employers, they were not heard and these people ultimately had to resign from post. One employee, a social worker, was so concerned, she acted differently, she collected the evidence she needed, and then resigned. Such was the horror that she witnessed, she was unable to remain in post.

These horrors involved an investigation by her and a colleague into the children within the boroughs care homes and the difficulties that they experienced when checking on the children's welfare. In interviews the children were described as 'deeply depressed and 'rocking back and forth, crying all the time' the inability of the children to articulate their problems led the two to delve further. On collecting her evidence, the whistleblower now had a dilemma.

Knowing that she would not be heard in her profession, she was now faced with the difficulty of anywhere she chose to work would likely be headed by someone in the network. Paedophiles, protected by the anti harassment policy were moving freely around the management tier, with clean employment records they remained largely unchallenged. The press, however, were uncovering the facts as part of an investigation of their own. When the story broke, it would go on to fuel five separate investigations. In 1992 Margaret Hodge, whilst not accepting blame, stepped down to take a job with the accountancy firm Price Waterhouse.

It was now, Tony Blair as Prime Minister in office, for a second term, and in a later cabinet reshuffle he appointed his then neighbour, the former head of Islington Council, Margaret Hodge, as Minister for Children. So shocked were her former employees, about her appointment, it led one to comment that "it's like putting the fox in charge of the chickens". The whistleblower came forward and handed a dossier to The Metropolitan Police. Fast forward now to current day and the case is under review again as the investigations, that were all connected at the time by the 'network, are beginning to overlap with the evidence given to Tom Watson MP by Ex-NAYPIC employee Chris Fay and the Jimmy Saville Evidences.

The overarching theme in all of this is the 'irrefutable evidence' to suggest that an organised Paedophile Ring is alive and well and residing in government. This evidence is the 'Elm Guest House' evidence and refers to the meeting place for the network. The guest house, ran by Carol Kazir and her husband is to be revisited evidence for yet another costly inquiry, and an off shoot of the Peter Righton MP case and over lapping into the evidence of the Jimmy Saville enquiry. The use of the Guest house and its conference facilities are well described by Chris Fay in his interview and was well known about throughout government that formed many on its guest list. There is an excellent blog called www.ukpaedos-exposed.com. It show the guest book list and cites a list of the 120 councillors in privileged positions who have been convicted of child abuse and paedophilia.

The point to take from all this - is that the danger to our children doesn't always come from the street and those lurking near our park. The risks can stem from policy makers, officials, people in power and people with power, and the power to do something about it. The fact that they don't, the fact that they 'close ranks' to protect their own and fail to act, to the benefit of themselves, should rattle us all.

Because our attention is being diverted away from the root cause, looking to the street as the danger, when in reality the danger is far greater than we can realise.

We should be asking questions and demanding responses, that do in fact answer the questions, and we should not settle for the now familiar 'smoke and mirrors' response, or allow for the odd 'unequivocally or unreserved' apology, as being an adequate response.

Chapter Fourteen

Taking a Gamble with Gamble

Taking a Gamble with Gamble

When the Child Exploitation and Online Protection agency (CEOP) came into being in 2006, it was a choice move to install Jim Gamble as their Chief Executive.

He was, at the time, a well respected and key player in the CEOPs plan to work alongside both governmental and non-governmental organisations within the field.

What this man provided, according to his fans, was an array of 'no stone-unturned' methods. He was a straight talking, shoot-from-the-hip type. When he wanted something done, he was able to articulate exactly what it should like and the role or function it should play. This won him many admirers; in reality though, he had a few problems that he needed to address.

The first was the continually expanding online safety risk and the second was to address the disparity in services and responses to abducted and missing children, nationally. One example of addressing the online risks, that was to run and run, as if on a loop in the background, was the Facebook safety button. This well documented wrangle was due to what Jim Gamble knew to be the risks, which were an inability of an online generation to summon help and report abuse online, in a timely way, Versus Facebook and its desire to remain a business first and foremost.

They didn't feel the same need to address this safety issue in what was being promoted, by them, as a 'Social Network'.

Jim Gamble knew exactly how he wanted the site to operate in terms of a direct link or 'Button' to report online threats to the CEOP. However, Facebook did not see it that way. They did not see the need for something that according to them, it was already spending millions on, annually. Facebook spokesperson Joanna Shields, stated at the time that;

"nothing is more important than the safety of our users, which is why we have invested so much in making Facebook one of the safest places on the internet".

Facebook

Jim Gamble did not agree and the wrangle ended in a compromised deal in which the CEOP button would only be available to download to a users Facebook page in a bid to be a deterrent. This seemed like a workable solution but was a large step away from the original request of a 'Panic Button' appearing on every page. The Panic Button deal, albeit, a compromised one, was a done deal and Jim Gamble's CEOP was now addressing its second concern. Scoping the disparity of services already in 'the industry' and setting out what role the CEOP would play in 'plugging the gaps'.

The scoping report was an investigation into the services already working in the arena of either child abduction, missing children, online safety and child trafficking, collectively known as 'missing children'. In defining the nature of the problem, the report concluded that it was multi-faceted and was a broad, complex and challenging issue. It described the UK problem as "poorly defined, lacking in accurate statistic and subject to an array of responses at local, national and international levels" The scoping report was also a systematic review of what had already been reported on before, namely by the NSPCC, The Children's Society,

Barnardos and various academic studies. The aims of the report was to identify and address any key strategic threats arising from the findings, allowing the CEOP to set out its stall with accuracy.

It identified knowledge gaps, problems with the reporting and recording infrastructure within a fragmented Police Force. Some were using Hermes Data bases and others were using paper forms that were different at a local level and only partially filled out by some forces. This was reeking havoc with the ability to provide any cohesive figures on child abduction. The Hermes database was one of manual entry and the information held within it, was reliant on the ability of the inputting officer, in order to capture the much needed data scores.

The report also concentrated on defining the different types of missing children that were being collectively held under one 'umbrella term'. Of the many agencies outside the CEOP, the report also highlighted that these services were "fragmented and disorganised, lacking leadership and coordination" It referred to a 2006 survey by The Parliamentary All Party Group for Runaway and Missing Children – which incredibly, identified twenty three children's services departments (Government Led) that did not know how many children in their own care had been reported missing to the police, in the previous year. Even more shocking was that a separate forty two departments did not know how many children on their child protection register had been reported missing to the police in the same period.

What was becoming apparent was that the CEOP was carving a role for itself in an inherited, historically-fragmented service that was failing vulnerable children and worse still, it was haemorrhaging funds. The processes on missing children were failing at every post. The reporting, recording, disseminating, response to and actions were at best a postcode lottery. Lack of continuity on the focus of missing children was cited and a lack of national standards to approach the problem was another factor. Some of this responsibility lay at the Home Office Door and the report was certainly disseminated to them.

To the CEOP, this scoping report was seen as a key document in defining and shaping a response that would set out what the CEOP would do about it, how this would be done and within what time scale. The development of a strategy could not have been possible before and the CEOP needed strategy to be clear as it was about to become the National, Strategic and Operational Lead, on missing, abducted and trafficked children or collectively 'missing children'.

It was now 2010 and four years post in conception and Operation Ore was an ongoing project that had not delivered on its promises at this time. But certainly the VIP lists, a product from Operation Ore would have been known.

From the Scoping report came the identification of three key threats, these were Sexual Exploitation, Child Trafficking and Abducted Children. The report also highlighted that the responsibility for missing children's welfare rested firmly with the relevant children's services, despite their highlighted shortcomings. The report also provided the CEOP with a mission and from this a mission statement. This mission statement can be seen as;

Prevent, Protect and Pursue

This became their slogan and would appear on all their future documentation.

They then set out how this could be achieved and

how they would carry it out:
Prevent – with Education and Awareness
To develop educational resources to prevent the causes of why children go missing, for children, families and schools. To target delivery of the specialist education modules to vulnerable children who may or may not be in mainstream education, such as looked-after children or those with special needs. To consider broadening the youth panel arrangements to include children and young people who have had experience of going missing. To raise awareness for parents and carers on the risks of abduction. To coordinate national awareness campaigns to encourage children and young people to seek help in a culturally appropriate and sensitive manner.

Prevent – with Improving Online Resources
Develop a one stop approach to online resources for children, families and professionals, working with stakeholders both nationally and locally, including the use of the missing kids website. Build a coordinated approach with partners to public appeals on missing children. To support national appeals for missing children launched by other specialist agencies. Work with partners to develop enhanced ways of reaching-out to missing children using new media and digital services.Notwithstanding, other prevention measures that involved, training and development for professionals, strategic knowledge development, and tactical support and coordination. But it is the two prevention measures that relate to education and awareness, and improving online safety resources that upsets me the most. In their 58 page report, the CEOP then sets out what *it will do,* in its executive summary;"the new CEOP capability will provide:

Educational resources and awareness for children

and their parent/carers;

Training for the police;

Support to police operations through targeted research and analysis;

Operational support for forces and missing children by extending the CEOP 'one stop shop' to include online missing children resources;

And finally,

Assurances that coordination arrangements and capability are in place to manage complex or high profile missing children cases.

The issue I have is that families, or parents, just do not know, they are not risk aware, they could not correlate the measures that the CEOP claim as being in place and of their impetus. Of the one hundred families asked, there was not a single mention of the 'Think U Know' campaign and not a single mention of the CEOP as being one of those thought to be responsible, for anything they might know about child safety. This is a really poor state of affairs. The promises to make information accessible to parents – just hasn't happened. The single informational 'Hub' for parents is non-existent. Parents are not in the loop and remain woefully uninformed.

The disparity on perceived risk is demonstrable and parents are continuing to put their children in danger.

The much hyped, based on 'even bad publicity is publicity' analogy of the CEOP's panic button remains a mystery to parents. The much needed "revamp" of the 'Stranger Danger' message cited by the CEOP themselves as both inadequate and outdated (CEOP Command Press Release 2011) has not been revamped.

Nothing has been done and parents continue to cite this 'Stranger Danger' message as the number one of 'what they know and would chose to pass on to their children'.

This relic of advice has been a revamp project of the CEOP for 2 years now.

Parents are completely in the dark when it comes to the known risks and the CEOPs claim that their message is on target is simply wrong and not tested. If the risks are known about and that the 'at risk groups' have been known about for some time; an example being, the now known risk of teenage girls walking alone, lets say from school and that the increased risk of attempted abduction is from predators, arriving in, alighting from or being near their cars – why hasn't this been disseminated to parents? The lack of any information, disseminated to the public, or those actually at risk, therefore, really cannot be claimed as a success, can it?

I think that the CEOPs practice is highly questionable, in terms of both results, and its annual spend. I suspect that as parents, we are not the only ones left feeling frustrated by their broken promises. What other possible reasons could there be for some very public comments from the non-governmental agencies.

In their three year strategy - document the CEOPs opening gambit, after the prevent, protect and pursue branding has been stamped on us, is their reiterated focus for "ensuring that every child matters, everywhere" Well, I think they have failed and the views of the average British families that we surveyed, reflects this.

In a sea of acronyms, that are the various government bodies or off-shoots from the national strategic leads, and we have so far identified at least ten. Comes the very confusing document by the SVACV – The Sexual Violence Against Children and

Vulnerable People National Group - Which states that it works across government departments to;

"urgently address any missed opportunities to protect children and vulnerable people" SVACV

They conclude in their National Group Progress Report and Action Plan, that is under the ministerial direction of Rt Hon Damian Green MP, that their national agenda and forthcoming action plan is to be implemented across the various government departments and will name those accountable. On point 34 the government SVAVC state that they will "expand CEOPs missing children's function to include creation of a national child abduction hub to develop policy and provide information on child abduction for the public and professionals alike" This, the report claims will be delivered no later than October 2013 – *FAILED*.

It further states the 'hubs' agenda, also deliverable by October 2013, will;

Agree a UK-definition of child abduction – *FAILED*

Create a means of identifying all incidents of child abduction and attempted child abduction reported to police forces – *FAILED*

Harness opportunities to collect survey data on child abduction from children and/or parents – *FAILED*

Expand research into child abduction through partnerships with e.g: Universities – *NOTHING FOUND*

Publish an annual summary of statistics on child abduction – *FAILED*

Create a publicly accessible 'One Stop Shop' for information on child abduction – *FAILED*

ISBN: 978-1-78246-228-6

The level of these failings to deliver on what was, government set promises, is staggering and detrimental to all UK children. The risk of not having a working definition of UK child abduction has been known about for more than ten years. This is just unacceptable and unforgivable.

We should now be asking the following questions;
What could be the reason?
And,
Who and why are they beneficiaries of not having a working definition?

If those in government overseeing these organisations are failing, then who if anyone is overseeing them and what is their agenda?................It's time.

So, when Theresa May announced changes to the CEOP, by bringing it into alignment with the National Crime Agency (NCA) Its Chief Executive Officer, Jim Gamble, resigned. Whether it was the failure to maintain control over what he saw as his directional input, or whether his position was made untenable by the magnitude of the CEOP failings to parents, that he couldn't abide, is a matter for debate. And despite him having internet bloggers criticising his every move, he will remain a tremendous loss to the CEOP.

As for his relationship with the McCanns, he has also been under the spotlight and there has been a barrage of negative online blogs suggesting he held an inappropriate relationship with the couple. There is talk of the McCanns 'abuse of power' and them having CEOP manuals for internal use only, found in an apartment or their holiday home. I found nothing to suggest this as wrong doing.

We have to remember that the McCanns are educated people and educated people do not sit about quietly in a crisis. The manuals in their possession were simply the same scoping documents and publications that I found very easy to access. What I can say is that the time line and trail of the numerous studies and documents is mammoth and in a bid to understand the bigger picture, I have had to research most of them. I could have filled a holiday home with the CEOP files that I have had to read. It is not fair to make assumptions on two distraught and educated individuals who would do all they could to bring themselves up to speed and be in a position to understand and contribute to help find their child.

We should, as parents and fellow Britons, be ready to support the McCanns if the Michael Shrimpton claims, on Madeline's whereabouts, are correct; as that will be a very dark day for us all. That is all I am going to say on this, except I wish them well for the future and now freshly exposed as people in glass houses, we really shouldn't be throwing stones.

Chapter Fifteen

'The Camel's Back is About to Get it's Final Straw'

The Camel's Back is About to Get its Final Straw

There is something very big happening in the background, it's already started and, albeit slowly, it is gathering momentum. The government is about to have its very own *Landslide*. I predict that the fallout will be massive. So massive in fact that it will dwarf all other enquiries and could well, by its very nature, bring down the house.

What will probably happen though, is something similar to what is happening already, in that anyone who feels they are in the know, and are prepared to speak out; is having their reputations destroyed. The cause of this landslide is the very operation that was so ceremoniously paraded around the BBC Channels to the public as 'Smashing Organised Paedophile Rings in the UK'.

The fall out from Operation Ore will not go away quietly, however hard the government try to archive it. The reason for this is the very evidence that was set to cleanse the UK of its mass paedophile threat is actually the evidence that has the power to destroy it and the government of any of its remaining credibility.

The landslide set to engulf us all is gathering pace and the pressure is beginning to show. When the MP Tom Watson – who gave us the Murdoch and Phone Hacking scandal – stood up in Prime Ministers Questions on 24th October this year and asked for an enquiry into evidence that he stresses was not properly examined we felt a bit more of the Landslide. This evidence that he refers to relates to, and he states; "clear intelligence of a powerful paedophile network linked to parliament and Number 10" The stooge at the centre of this ring or the person suspected of supplying MPs with a regular stream of young boys; was the BBC presenter Sir Jimmy Saville. Now we have an interesting situation with more than one enquiry set to collide with the Operation Ore findings. The evidence from Ore comprises of a list of credit card holders and many are high profile UK figures, who would be revealed if this list is made public. The Saville Enquiry also has some of the same people named and now we have the same names yet again emerging from the evidence that MP Tom Watson is suggesting was not fully investigated.

Celebrities to are joining in with the 'piling on of pressure' with Philip Schofield handing over to David Cameron, live on This Morning, a piece of paper with a list of names of those parliamentarians considered to be involved. The evidence suggested to be in the possession of MP Tom Watson has been handed over to the Metropolitan Police to be "taken seriously". The list of names have already been published on the internet see them at www.cigpapers.wordpress.com

Several of them are serving politicians although one or two are now disgraced on other matters and have been relegated to the world of publishing their memoires, all of which have failed to inform us on these allegations. The recent publication of Edwina Currie's memoires is an exception and does go further with the allegations of the much known about, within government circles, of MP Peter Morrison's inappropriate relations with teenage boys.

Peter Morrison's conduct is a good example of the level to which this landslide has been covered up at every opportunity. His questionable conduct continued once out of parliament and this led the public to complain several times of his alleged loitering in public toilets. Twice arrested for his acts of 'cottaging' he was released without charge and escaped with a caution. The police arrest log was claimed to be missing and the distaste of his 'above the law treatment' was leaked to the press. You might think that a disgruntled member of the public went on to leak the story but it was in fact the arresting officers who later went on to tell the press of having their knuckles rapped for bringing him to book in the first place.

The reason we didn't get to hear about it, according to former editor of the Sunday Times (Peter Connew) was that the news paper was silenced on threats of libel. Still this has not stopped our disgruntled public from putting it on the net. And the appropriately named net is closing in. Rod Richards the former conservative MP and Ex-Leader of the Welsh Tories made further allegations about Margaret Thatchers closet advisor. He cites Sir Peter Morrison's *many* trips to two welsh care homes, Bryn Estyn and Bryn Allen Hall, were well known about and that he did not act alone.

Other cases include the Scandal at Haut de la Garrene the Jersey childrens home. Young boys were picked up from the home by their frequent visitor Sir Jimmy Saville and delivered to Ted Heath, former Prime Minister, for sailing trips aboard his yacht. The difference, it is claimed, is that these boys never returned. Missing presumed murdered – the enquiry led to the digging up of the care home grounds.

No bodies were ever found.

Michael Shrimpton, the Barrister and National Security Expert - cites these murders on the yacht as common place and known to Sir Jimmy Saville at the time he further suggests that the weight of these child murders, being one reason for Sir Jimmy's sudden return to faith shortly before he died. He also raises the question – how was it possible not to act on the 450 crimes committed by Saville, until after his death, if it was not part of a cover up? This was in an interview with Bristol Community Radio aired on January 11th 2013 (listen to that interview at, www.bcfmradio.com) He also claims that Madeline McCann was abducted to order and that MI6 know who it is as does Mr Shrimpton and on his excellent blog he also suggests that there has been a conspiracy or witch hunt to blame the McCanns for a murder that could not have been carried out by them, but that Madeline has been dead since 2008. His rationale for this is well explained. You can access his blog at www.theshrimptonblog.com .

Another sordid tale is that of the incident at Lord Brittan's home when a young boy was found staggering half naked from his house. The former Home Secretary to Margaret Thatcher was investigated and according to internet sources the boys were paid off to keep them quiet. Lord Brittan's punishment – he was called in front of William Hague and told that he could not remain in UK politics. He was made a commissioner for the UK and allowed to stay in Jersey until corruption investigated in the Compton Enquiry outed him.

The list of Parliamentarians involved and already named is immense and it is almost now a process of elimination to work out who could possibly be left to form yet another list. Here is the list of those convicted www.uk-paedos-exposed.com

This list, However, does not include those who have conveniently had their arrests or cautions covered up. This leaves us, as parents, with some very difficult questions.

Questions:

Are those charged with the well paid positions of protecting our children from paedophiles, themselves paedophiles?

Is our Government an established Paedophile ring of untouchables, that have a vested interest in not forming a definition of Child Abduction or enforcing the findings of countless enquiries to record this data correctly?

Are the inappropriate names given to the Government and Police Inquires into abducted children such as 'Taken' and the title used for missing children namely 'Throwaways' just the type of terms and values placed on children by Paedophiles?

When the truth is outed will the Government give the families whose lives have been destroyed, for looking at images that may not of been child pornography, an apology?

Will the Government give its people a definition to clarify the difference between the illegal act of looking at an inappropriate image on a home computer versus, sending a government Jaguar to pick up an under age boy for paid sex with a minister for parliament, which appears to be legally acceptable?

How will the Government now convince parents that it is fully behind it's slogan of "every child matters"?

How will the Government assure its people that it operates with transparency?

The recent case of Ben Fellows is about to hit the fan, Listen out for it, at the time of this investigations close; Ben was arrested and charged with Conspiracy to Pervert the Course of Justice following his allegations of sexual assault made against an MP; to see this google ben fellows.

He was called to Charring Cross Police station to give a witness statement only to be arrested and have his house stripped bare of its wireless technology in a bid to discredit him. The case is at present unresolved and he is in talks with a leading national newspaper. What is interesting is his secret footage and his police interviews that were covertly recorded by the now fearful, bailed man, you can see this on the link provided.

The level of fear from the pressure of being involved is also being felt by MP Tom Watson whose comments on his blog suggest that he has left a trail for the evidence he has passed on 'in case anything should happen to him'. Whilst the actions of Philip Schofield on This Morning have been described in the press as clumsy what has been achieved is a very public trail and whilst those involved will be protected and moved in to other positions and probably made into a good will ambassadors or given diplomatic roles, the problem will now not go away. If the brush that sweeps does its job correctly then one might ask, when the job is done who will be left to run the country?

The problem appears to be inherent, widespread and systematically embedded in the culture of the elite who believe it is their right to remain well paid, untouchable and above the very laws they are empowered to protect. How else could they justify the running of a 'Dirt Book?'

The Introduction of the Dirt Book.

When I found about this, I just couldn't believe it, I wanted to go round there like an angry parent and tell them off. I imagined I would have to climb up in a tree house and a lot of sculky school boys in shorts would all lower their heads until I applied enough pressure and one of them would then hand over a hastily scrolled, tatty, barely legible, black book containing some idiotic fantasies they had all dreamt up in their spare time. But then, I remembered these are not silly school boys, these are the people we are paying to run our country. So I will just have to remain....i don't know really, shocked.... I suppose.

The dirt book is the record kept by the Chief Whip in the House of Commons and is said to be a black book that notes all the wrong doings and paedophile activities of those 'caught out' in the act and is used by the Chief Whip as a form of control or extortion over the MPs contained within it. First introduced by Ted Heath for his Whip - Tim Fortescue - (1970-1973) who himself leaked the information to the BBC in their Documentary – Westminster's Secret Service (2005) it contained all those whose activity and inappropriate relations with young boys was known about and covered up within parliament.

Now even more worrying than the fact that it has been used to cover up and bribe the Members whose details are contained within it, it was also used as a method for grooming and promoting MPs within the House as 'a better control could be kept on them and their activities' For the first time there is evidence that paedophilia was both encouraged and was more likely to lead to promotion within the house. If that is true then the questions raised by Tom Watson MP, about an 'Established, Organised, Paedophile Ring' would certainly have some weight to it.

The evidence of Elm Guest House, the alleged parliamentary paedophile brothel, frequented by Ministers must form part of this evidence and as those in elite positions continue to retire, more is becoming known. The Dirt Book, it's claimed, has been discontinued. But there is still evidence for its plausible existence in the comments of those well respected retires, such as Police Officer McLachlian, who played a key role in Operation Ore suggesting that paedophilia is still not a priority on the Home Office's National Policing Plan and that Governments claims of a prioritisation was merely a 'smoke and mirrors' response. With the plans to proceed on Operation Ore looking more like a go slow through lack of funding we have to ask the question that with so many delays to arrest those exposed by the ore data; how much of the delays can now been seen as a tactic to allow those on ' the VIP list' to destroy their evidence? As McLachlain points out if those in high places cling tightly to their collections of images and home computers (expected to be up to ten years old) then they only have themselves to blame. But realistically, how much tangible evidence will be left out there? And how difficult will it now be to recover?

It would now seem that the delay tactic has in fact closed the window of opportunity to act on the evidence and Ore will be relegated to yet another parliamentary scandal at the cost of the public and its much squeezed funds.

The much talked about list of VIPs in Government circles will for now, remain the property of a leading national newspaper. Whether the newspaper is not publishing the list as was the plan, because of a D-Notice in place is a matter for debate. But a list certainly exists as part of the Operation Ore evidence.

Chapter Sixteen

Your To Do List

Your To Do List
   1: Make a TO DON'T List.................. TODAY.
   Your To Don't List
   Don't Get Stuck in Normal

Here's a snap shot of your modern parenting life, I've based this on mine and you might find some similarities with your own life. Have you ever thought about who's deciding normal these days? Is it the Government, Religion, TV, Trade and Industry, Our Peers or Our Neighbours? The list is endless. When do the things that creep into our life become normal? Exactly when did it become normal to buy a new sofa every 10 minutes? Really, those adverts are on all the time. And when did we start comparing everything? Soon we will need a compare site to compare our compare sites. Why *do* we drive two miles away from our local high street just to have free parking and a weekly shop that is a few pence cheaper (providing you buy fifty of the same thing and then throw half of it away). Only to blow all your savings while you sit bumper to bumper trying to get out of the free car park without going around and around and ending up in an impromptu car wash.

You get home and compare the receipt online with a rival supermarket and claim back the .47 pence difference that you could have saved had you been prepared to shop somewhere you didn't want to go in the first place, that is two miles in the opposite direction, and that's just the shopping. Our lives are getting complicated and complications equal less time – less time with our children. When we finally get up to the house we live in (I say live....) that is complicated too.

We get told when the street lights will go off, when we will get our bin emptied and when the water will be cut-off for essential repairs. We find out about these essential repairs because there is a road sign telling you that the road, that your tiny house is on, is now inaccessible and just because you've paid a cool quarter of million for the tiny thing, you will now need to carry all your shopping the length of the street and you probably live at number 110 and not 10. You finally get inside to find a large bill for all these privileges that you should pay direct to your local authority.

If you dispute the bill you get an answerphone – normal, if you don't pay the bill you get a court order to pay – normal, if you don't pay this in time you'll get a court case heard in your absence (they don't need you for this) – normal. The once unaffordable bill becomes an unaffordable court fine plus costs – normal; and if you don't pay this then they'll cut off your means to pay it by clamping your car or sending someone round to seize your goods for ten times the value of the court fine – all normal.

It seems the only thing more tedious than all of this is trying to get a doctors appointment, because now you're not feeling very normal. When did all this become normal?

Well....... Let Me Tell You.

It all became normal at about the same time as driving the kids to school on two wheels, while they eat their breakfast on the back seats of the car that you have hardly started paying for yet. You arrive at school just in time for them to join a queue of thirty other children, with breakfast slopped all down their jumpers and as you wave them off into the government institution, that you know is getting it wrong but you just hope that they'll survive the day, and at best fail to be noticed because they are normal, you can then breathe a sigh of relief as your parental responsibility is over for six hours. You stay in the playground just long enough to be snubbed by the 'stay-at-home- all-dayers' headed up by Judy who runs mums, bums and tums or some other crap and then you wheel spin off to join a traffic jam. where you'll now sit for 45 minutes behind a lorry, smoke endless cigarettes if you can afford them while you listen to the radio or 'The Morning Crew' ('It's not a boat') where everyone sounds really happy or they are on drugs.

When you get to work there is nowhere to park so you sit picking Cherrios off of the report that you said you would take home the night before, because there are not enough hours in the day that you actually get paid for, only to give half of it back to the government that then pays a 'quango' or 'think tank' to come up with phrases like 'unequivocally sorry' for when the whole thing goes 'turd side up'. Well that was my life anyway, before I kicked it to the kerb.

Seriously though, things have gotten out of control and we now live in a 'look but don't see' or at best a 'see but don't have time to do anything about it' society.

And yes it's one that we have created and yes it's one whose social problems we will ultimately end up paying for (remember that 4 Trillion Pound estimate).

The best thing you can do is don't. Did you get that, i'll say it again.

The Best Thing You Can Do is....Don't

Don't get stuck in Normal – it isn't working, the time you need to spend with your children is now and nothing can buy back that time.

To find out if you are a parent stuck in Normal –

try this questionnaire
Questions

1: Have you ever answered your mobile phone whilst on the toilet?

2: Gone to work in odd socks or even odd shoes?

3: Put make up whilst driving?

4: Taken your child to school when it wasn't even open? *(The inset day error!)*

5: Forgot your child or spouses birthday/anniversary? *(this includes leaving the present at work or on the roof of your car!)*

6: Fallen asleep and missed your stop on a bus or train?

7: Forgot to attend an appointment that you yourself made only a few days before?

8: Do you know your child's shoe size without looking?

9: The name of their best friend or TV character?

10: The name of their school teacher and how to spell it?

11: What they had for dinner yesterday?

12: Have you recently forgotten to feed your pet?

SCORES – 2 points per question

0-6: Sterling work parent, pat yourself on the back - not when you are driving though – that would be madness.

6-12: Easy..... Careful.....You could be heading for the trap, the trap that you don't see until you're hanging upside down by one leg, and everyone can see your pants.

12-20: Oh dear, I can see you hanging there by one leg and I suppose you want me to come and cut you down don't you? Well sorry I'm too busy you'll have to ask John in accounts.

20-24: Oh Dear you better check your self before you wreck yourself and everyone else around you for that matter, including your children, elderly relatives and possibly the neighbours cat!!!

Don't Lose Your Marbles

I have 78 marbles until one of my sons becomes 16 and I know that when he becomes 16 he will probably have left home and gone to University. So every weekend I am losing a marble. I keep these marbles in a jar on the Kitchen windowsill as a visual reminder of how long we have left together. I did this after reading a really nice story in a book.

A busy working dad realised he was so busy that he was missing most of his children's lives and in particular his daughter who was growing fast. He realised that his time would continue to melt away unless he could find a way of slowing it down.

He went out and bought some marbles and when he got home he carefully counted out 143 into a jar. He had 143 Saturdays left with his daughter before she went to College. Each Saturday he removed one marble to remind him visually of the importance of investing his time in his daughter before she left. He knew that it was inevitable that he would lose his marbles but now he had the chance to decide how he would lose them.

They spent these Saturday mornings together, talking, walking, doing things together, the things that mattered. It was their time. It doesn't matter what you do it just matters - that you do.

Note to Reader: If you get time read Weird by Craig Groeschel – he's an American Preacher, but if you think you cant get past that, think again, he writes really well and his words are melody when you are ready to hear them..... He speaks about normal and also cites this marble story as one to pay attention to. You can access his work at www.zondervan.com/ebooks

Enjoy Every Marble.............There is no time like NOW.

Don't be a Myth Teller

I'm not talking about the one 'if the wind changes your face will stay like that' or 'If you don't eat your greens you will get hairy legs' they are just for fun and I am sure that a bird in your hand probably is worth two in the bush. I mean the ones that are harmful or those myths that are said without any explanation. The ones we use when we don't have the time to explain what we mean. We have been programmed with these myths by the generations before us, just like magic-e in school or singing your times tables and when they get called into play our brain delivers them. They roll off the tongue and instantly they do their job of stopping the conversation dead.

As parents we use them like trump cards that can't be trumped. They can't be trumped because our children just don't understand them. These mythical sentences do not get explained and our children get the cue to shut up but they don't get the lesson.

'don't judge a book by its cover' usually accompanied by a wagging finger!

It's unbelievable we use them like get out of jail free cards or vay-nights. The more you look for them in times of stressful conversation the more you see them; and you see them in some pretty high powered places too; Politicians speeches, Police Statements and government announcements.

I was at work one day in a busy Accident & Emergency Department, I was one of several senior staff on that day but not the one in charge. A mother came busting through the doors looking for her nine year old daughter who had been at Brownie Camp. It was the last day and the Brownies were having a barbecue. As they all stood in line waiting for their food the gas powered barbecue had exploded; children were being brought in with burns, shrapnel injuries and smoke inhalation and as we were the nearest hospital we were on major incident alert. The mother was clearly distressed she had tried to phone the Brownie Leader but could not get through and decided to come straight down to the hospital. This is typical of any parent in this situation and I would have done exactly the same.

The Sister on shift that day had been tasked with the press releases and information giving. After taking the name of the child she checked her list of casualties brought in so far and told the mother "your daughter has not been brought into the hospital at this time". This did not appease the distraught mum, who now wanted to know what this statement meant; did it mean that her daughter wasn't injured or did it mean that she was so badly injured that she wasn't a priority.

The situation began to get a little heated.

The Sister stayed calm and said "we are the only hospital taking casualties from this incident and your daughter isn't here, and regardless of the level of any injuries, she would be brought here". Now that probably would have been enough, she could have stopped right there but she didn't, she was about to get some help from one of our friends. Just as her statement finished she then said "so no news is good news at this stage". Then something strange happened, there was a deadly silence in the department and I'm sure that someone, somewhere, stopped playing a piano. It was as if there was no way back, no opening in the dialogue, it was an absolute conversation stopper. The mother stood for a moment open mouthed and then burst into tears and fell on her knees... it was pretty horrendous. Her daughter was in fact fine and had not been injured in the incident.

When you work at a senior level in this field, you are given adequate training in communicating bad news at any level and you get numerous times to practice it.

The culprit here was our "no news is good news" friend that went and tagged itself on the end of the sentence. Be aware of them when you are talking to your children. Remember they come in times of high pressure or emotive subjects, they tag themselves on the end of your sentence and they are the work of your subconscious mind - actually your subconscious mind wants out of the conversation and can't wait for your permission. They are a blunt and useful tool but only in the right places.

Test It Out on Someone....if you dare!

Your friend comes over and is boring you about her 'partner problems' you like your friend but you don't want to spend the whole morning talking about this sort of thing so you allow her to get into full flow...there's a natural pause where she expects a response from you or maybe just a look and that's when you do it..... you give her the bomb... why not...after all it's not you doing it, distance yourself from it further by saying something like "well you know what they say... you made your bed, you better lie in it" BLAM... bomb delivered. Then look at her and smile sweetly see what she does next.....chances are she does nothing...just stares back at you... bewildered. It's a conversation cul-de-sac and if they are very communication savvy they might voice their distaste but it will be mild at best.

Meanwhile their subconscious mind will be bringing up the drawbridge and battening down the hatches and they won't ever talk about it, to you, again. A bit mean and not for the faint hearted...perhaps keep it for a party when your get trapped in the kitchen with someone who really is boring you.

The point to take from all of this is that if these mythical bombs bounce into your conversations with your children, retract them immediately, correct them and definitely take the time to explain them. It's a damage limitation exercise.

Some other examples of Myth's you might try to avoid using with your children and take the time to explain to them.

"Children should be seen and not heard" - A bit too much like being on a Laptop!

"Best to be on the safe side" - which side is that then exactly?

"Lightning never strikes twice" - It does... you can see it on Youtube.

"Familiarity breeds contempt" – Hmmm...what?

"Out of sight, out of mind" - No, I think that means Lost or Forgotten.

"Practice what you preach" - Unless you're a drugs councillor!

"One good turn deserves another" – No, just a thank you is enough.

"Never judge a book by its cover" - Then what's the point of having a cover?

"A problem shared is a problem halved" followed by the mother of all reactions when they do tell you their problem it's probably the worst thing you can do.

Don't Leave Their Survival to Chance
'Just a Shirt Button from Death'

Some years ago in America, an eight year old boy was walking home from school. On this day his short journey did not take its normal route there was a fire in one of the many disused buildings and the fire crew had closed the road. It was winter, four thirty in the afternoon and the daylight was beginning to fade.

The boy was not fazed as this was his neighbourhood and he knew every road and route home. He passed by back yards, side alleys and back alleys on a route that took him around the block and past his local park. The park was a small patch of wasteland between two tenement buildings that the local parents had brought back to life. There was a swing, a bench and a basket ball hoop but on this day the park was empty, most children had already headed home for their supper.

Parked outside the park entrance was a man in a car, his window slightly open. He struggled with a map book. Frustrated, he turned the pages back and fourth from one to another. As the young boy passed the car, the man called to him.

"hey sonny what's the name of this street?"

He gestured, using his finger to point up and down the road.

'"Jefferson Street" the boy replied.

"What did you say son?....I can't hear you my window is stuck up and all"

The boy moved closer to the car so that the man could hear him.

"Jefferson Street Sir" he said again.

"Jepherson Street?"... The man sat higher in the drivers seat to talk through the gap in his broken window.

"and where does it go after that sonny?"

"It crosses Baille and Maine" the boy said with confidence.

"Oh my' said the man *'that just can't be"*...he was now shaking his head. The man started again.

"You know I could be wrong here but...am I even on

the right street?" he began rubbing his forehead.

The boy moved closer to the car as he could see this man was in trouble...he was plain lost.

The man sat up to speak through the gap in the window again only this time he dropped the map book down on the floor of the car and then opened the door to retrieve it. He quickly found the page he was on and turned the map book so that the boy could look at the page, and the boy moved closer. The man held the map book up with one hand flat underneath it and the boy pointed to the small patch of grass on the map that was the park.

Without any warning the man used his free hand and grabbed the boys clothing around his neck and pulling him close, he head butted him. In a second he had pulled the boys body across his and into the car. Shoving him down into the passenger footwell where he punched him a couple more times. He closed the car door, threw down the map book, put up his window and drove off.

Now, at this point I know you probably don't want to read any further but it's not because you don't care about this eight year old boy. It's because you can see just how easy it is or more importantly just how easily it could be your eight year old child. The same eight year old that you have primed to *"always be kind to others"* or *"think about how others might feel"* or what about *"help those less fortunate than yourself"* and lest we forget *"always treat people as you would want to be treated"*.

The only single overriding message we ever tell them is **"don't talk to strangers"**.

Then we do it all the time.

When we are out with our children, we ask for directions, talk with strangers at the bus stop, outside shops, in cues and the list is endless. If we see someone being odd we relay the story later to our partner or friends, it was funny "that person was so out there and they were doing the funniest thing; everyone in the cue was laughing...huhh if you'd of seen it you would have laughed; it was funny right kids?

Ask yourself another question; when you told your child "if someone makes you feel uncomfortable you have to tell an adult" How long did you spend explaining what uncomfortable meant or what it might feel like? Here's another couple; when we chat openly in front of our children and say something like "that person looked really dodgy" Did you take any time to explain what dodgy is? How many of us can really say that we've had the conversations we need to have with our children?

"the conversations that might one day save their life!"

Now read on because this is no ordinary eight year old boy. Paulie was an eight year old boy who's mother was a Police Officer and she had, had those conversations with her son. Paulie had been primed to act, he had a plan and it had been imprinted on him.

Paulie lay on the passenger footwell floor face down. When he came to he knew he was on the move, and on his way to the second scene.

Lesson Number One

"Never let someone take you to the second scene.

The second scene is where they will do everything they are unable to do to you in the first. If you get to the second scene, chances are that you're never coming back.

Paulie began wiping the blood from his face on the carpet, he pulled fibres from the carpet and put them in his mouth and ears. The man, now alerted to him being awake pulled him up on to the passenger seat and told Paulie to put on his seat-belt. Handing the boy a dirty cloth he told him to 'clean up his face'. Paulie began to spit on the cloth and wipe it on his face and a couple of times he faked a sneeze', forcefully he spat blood and spit, his DNA, all over the dashboard of the car.

The car was driving fast and Paulie knew that his chances of ever coming back were slim and that something bad was going to happen. He had started the routine his mother had taught him and he knew that he must not give up and that what he was doing may or may-not save him, but it might tell his mother where he was.

Lesson Number Two
"Five things I know about you and Personalise Yourself."

Paulie began to make a mental note of five things he could know about this man, that the man could not easily change. The colour of his eyes, the shape of his ears, the width of his neck, shape of his teeth and TABS; Tattoo's, Anything odd, Birthmarks & Scars. Then he began to personalise himself, giving himself a name, making stuff up and making up conversation. He said things like "I've been to school today, I played soccer and I scored the only goal – I like soccer but I don't like swimming – my little sister likes swimming though" The man became agitated and told Paulie to quit it. He then launched into the next phase 'apologising' "sorry.. I do this a lot my mom says quit it too, did your mom ever tell you that?... sorry you must get this a lot right?" Paulie was dropping conversation bombs wherever he could, forcing the man to recall past events and family members. Then he suddenly stopped talking to allow the man to think about everything he had just said.

Lesson Number Three
"Know where you are and what you have."

Paulie began to check the car, window winders and handles were on, door was locked and the button was present. The car was a Sedan it said so on the steering wheel and it was being driven with a key. There was hardly any fuel in the car so they couldn't be going far. There was the map book on the back seat but nothing else stood out. The car was noisy, the engine had trouble and was working hard. The road was dark, but it was a main road, there was tarmac under the wheels.

Some time further along the road the man said *"I'm going to stop and get some gas, you sit tight and keep quiet and nothing bad will happen to you"* He gave Paulie a hard stare, and Paulie nodded. The man pulled into a petrol garage forecourt and got out and locked the car with the key. He began to walkover to the barrels of ready made gas. Paulie watched his walk, he walked with a limp. Paulie fiddled with his clothes he knew that he didn't have much time. The man paid the forecourt attendant and picked up the Jerry-Can full of Gas. Paulie took his chance.

Lesson Number Four
"Use what you have."

Paulie took a button from his shirt by turning it and wedged it in the ignition barrel of the car. The man opened the car door and flung the Jerry-Can on the back seat he then tried to put the key in the ignition. He was confused and couldn't understand why the key would not go in and looked closely down the barrel. Paulie, had undone his seatbelt in readiness and in the confusion the man had not locked door from the inside. Paulie flung open the door and ran.

Lesson Number Five
"Shout what you know will work and use words

that don't fit."

Paulie ran across the petrol forecourt and as he did he was pulling off his clothes and throwing them to the floor. He shouted "FIRE", The petrol attendant opened the door and rushed to help him, Paulie ran past him and into the building.

He shouted to the petrol attendant *"that man has abducted me, he's a stranger, my mum is a police officer and her number is officer 457"*. He then anchored himself to the bottom of the counter and the petrol attendant locked the door and called to his wife who was out the back. She called the police.

In an interview later, the petrol forecourt attendant said *"I knew this boy wasn't faking it, no small boy uses a word like abduction... I did what I could"*. The car was abandoned on the forecourt and although the man was not caught straight away his DNA was recovered from the car and the map book and he was apprehended at a later date.

Paulie made it back from the second scene and he never gave up, he was awarded a bravery award and his story was published in the local press with a picture of him and his very proud mother.

Paulie wasn't a big or particularly strong boy, but he had been primed to act...and he knew what to do. I want my sons to be like Paulie and I want my son's sons and daughters to be like Paulie... because the second scene option just doesn't bare thinking about. It's a gift I'm giving them and we work on it.....a lot.

Don't Let Them Fail

How can you help your children in today's society, when it seems that they are living in times, unsupported? When considering danger, children do not have the ability to make the same judgements that adults do, and for them it occurs in phases. Younger children do not know, older children think that they know, but they don't. Teenagers don't want to know. This alone makes it difficult for parents to know where to begin.

As parents, we won't always get it right and it doesn't matter that we don't know where to begin, but it does matters that we do begin, somewhere. Below are some examples of practical measures you can use to protect your children. You will see that some might leave you with the feeling that they are too extreme, and that fine. But I have included all of them so that you can then choose, what is appropriate for you and your family. It's not a science, and you could make-up some of your own.

Using the "Is It Wise" Method

Your teenager is enthusiastic (*possibly, not seen for a while*) about going to a friends house to stay over. You know this friend and for you it is an easy decision and you say yes, without hesitation. You later discover that the parents of your teenager's friend will not be at home and to make matters worse the friend has invited some others, and you don't know who they are. Initially you might jump at the chance to get your teenager out of the house, if only to have the sofa back for a short period and watch something you would like to watch, for a change. To this request you say yes. But is it wise?

By using this technique something strange happens, there is a shift from considering the situation internally or just within the household, to applying the problem globally, it then becomes a wider issue and much more easy to answer because you are not relying on the emotion you have attached to your child. It is strange because the answer pops up immediately – somewhere in the parenting computer, you already have a firm and fixed opinion about this.

So what you are actually asking is, *Generally, is it wise for teenagers to be alone in a house together?* The answer then changes to No.

Try It, it has worked with every decision that I have ever had to make.

Pre-School to Pre-Teenage Children

Is it wise to: Lose sight of young children when out in public?

Is it wise to: Allow young children to use public toilets, unless they are going in with an adult?

Is it wise to: Leave your children in a parked car, if you are getting petrol ?

Advice

The actual advice given to parents is to always take their children with them.

But this is the real world and that is never going to happen. Car seats being what they are – difficult, and sweets all over the shop – even more difficult, it is probably raining and besides you will only be quick. Until someone's credit card fails or they decide to do their weekly shop, in the now, not so convenient - convenience store.

So here is the next best advice, and using a workable solution stops you falling into a routine that might not be a conscious one.

If you are not intending to go into the shop and you intend to pay at the window, then park or wait for the nearest pump to the pay window, remove the keys and always lock them in, even if they are only a couple of feet away.

Is it wise to: Leave you child with a sitter without telling them what you expect?

Advice

Have house rules for Sitters, Nannies or Helpers.

Stick them on the wall, examples might be: Not to allow them to have friends over when you are not there.

If your babysitter has a boyfriend, he needs to stay away, she's there to do a paid job. I had a friend tell me about a babysitter who wanted her boyfriend over; to revise (*"yeah, they are still using that one!"*) My friend agreed that he could come if he came on a separate day to meet with the family. He seemed a very nice young man and all was well. Two months later on a separate occasion she came home to find a complete stranger sat on her sofa. The babysitter had changed her boyfriend, young love.....bless them.

Other Questions You Could Ask

Is it wise to: Leave your children with friends, family or clubs, if they don't know your rules?

Is it wise to: Send your child to the shop, alone, to run an errand or post a letter?

Is it wise to: Leave your child in an arcade, play area or gaming zone, alone?

Advice

These places are mind numbingly boring for the average adult, but predators know this all to well, when children are distracted by gaming machines or play areas, they are highly vulnerable. It is also an area that any predator with a few coins, can fit in. These places often have single people, without children, hanging around. Some are interested gamers, of course, but there are few places that predators can easily fit it and *this is* one of them.

Teach Your Children......Well
A Code Word

Chose a code word that only your child will know, tell their school or nursery that they have a code word. If someone tries to collect them from school it will be an added protection. There have been cases where young children have been collected from school by a predator, neighbour or ex-family friend. They tell both the teacher and the child that the mother or father sent them. If they had been sent by the child's mum or dad, they would know the same code word as the child.

That They Have Your Permission

We spend all of our children's lives telling them that they should be polite and respectful to others. We never give them permission to be different. But different situations require a different response. For very young children there is 'mummy and daddy politeness' and everyone else gets, something else. Older children need to be given permission to get out of a situation or be given the permission to fight back. It is really important that you give your child permission to 'fight for their life', without fear of reprisal. This is a huge deal for children, and is the crossing of a boundary that needs permission. Equally they need to learn that there is a distinct difference between your instruction and the instructions of others. They do not have to do what someone else tells them, If it doesn't feel right. Tell them you can and will deal with any fall-out later.

Teach Them What Uncomfortable Feels Like

You want them to know and recognise this feeling, it can have many presentations, stomach ache, sweating, butterflies in the stomach, the hairs on the back of their neck, goosebumps, a jolt from their conscience, a voice in the background – you can see that this is a difficult one, the measure of this feeling is subjective, or unique to them, so you need to identify it for them, what feelings do they get, when they themselves feel uncomfortable? You need to talk about it, often.

They need to recognise the feelings, recognise the signals early, what is the first sign or symptom that they get, and act on it, before it is too late.

Some of the advice I have seen suggests a 'Pants Rule', Firstly none of this was evidenced in the survey and parents cited 'The Green Cross Code' as their chosen memorable advice. The Acronym 'Pants' is P – is for Privates are Private and so on – It is a valiant attempt, but any child that finds themselves in a situation where they are bargaining in this way, with the N - in pants meaning - No means No, is in a difficult bind. My concern is that to get to this point children would have had many early warning signals of feeling uncomfortable that have been bypassed and they would now be in a very dangerous situation. This is much, much too late.

Teach Them To Trust Their Instincts

No matter what! - this was an innate ability they had and it would have first shown itself when they were about eight months old. After that we spent most of our time shoving them forward to be kissed or cuddled by people they were instinctively unsure of. If your child doesn't want their picture taken with Uncle John, then Uncle John doesn't get his picture, and they should not be made to feel bad about it.

Teach Them To Lock-On

This is making themselves heavy, awkward to pick up, or difficult to remove, because they have either locked-on to an object in order to make themselves heavier. This could be a chair, a door, a railing or their bicycle, all are good examples; Or they may need to change their shape or stance. Make a game out of it, reward them. If they were being taken, you want them primed and ready for action, immediately. Practice with your own car in the drive way – if they make themselves into a star shape they are actually very difficult to get into a car. You might get some funny looks, but it can be quite good fun. From experience, they are even harder to remove from a restaurant, with a chair attached, "good job boys xx"

Teach Them To Be Physical

In schools today children are taught, very early on, that there is 'No Physical'.

It just isn't acceptable any more. Teach them it at home, with the rules of when to use it. Can they get out of a headlock or escape from a tight hug? I had boys and they wrestled the house down. Some furniture got damaged and that was okay with me. They would sit on each other, pin each other to the floor, it was amazing to see how inventive they could be. It needs to be supervised and you don't want them literally trying to kill each other, there has to be some rules – but if they can learn each others vulnerable points then they are learning a highly valuable skill.

Teach Them About Props

Predators will often use props to reinforce what they are saying or doing, the puppy, the map book, a walking stick, the list is endless. The props can also be comments that specifically back up what the person is saying. Children need to be aware of them because they add weight to the child's decision making and they will not realise that it is happening. When we communicate with someone else we are aware of them, in their totality. If they are limping, it registers with us and we will not be aware of it. It is our subconscious mind assisting us. In the case of Paulie, the Map Book was key to his decision, that this man must be lost and that it was safe to move closer to the car. Recognising early signals of being uncomfortable and learning to recognise props is important to their critical thinking and decision making.

Teach Them to Use What They Have

In the example of Paulie, it is evident that he had

been given that direction and it was the difference between being taken and getting away. Using what they have is something they should be aware of. Practice regularly by discussing what tools they have, their voice, a pencil, coins, and of course buttons on their clothes.

Here are a couple of examples. The looking behind trick – teach your child to look behind someone stood in front of them – done convincingly, this could buy them a few seconds when the person has to look behind to check that there is nobody there. They can practice this on Uncle John, but he still isn't getting a picture.

Throwing a coin or a stone

Done correctly – a coin thrown behind someone will make them think that there is someone behind them or that someone is coming. here is a reaction in most people to look, when they hear a coin drop. There are many other examples.

Practice them regularly make a game out it, if they can get you to look you have to double the value of the coin.

Teach Them to Have a Voice – What to Say

Children don't need any help when it comes to shouting, standing on the peripheries of any birthday party or bouncy castle is proof enough, but it's what they shout that makes a difference. They need to be succinct, to the point, shouting help is not always beneficial and politeness has to be put aside too. They shouldn't waste time describing what is happening to them, "he's got me" or "they've got hold of my arm" is probably evident and won't help them. They need to shout a command to others. "Get Help...Now, I don't know this person, he's abducting me" they need to be specific and use words that do not necessarily fit well together or that do not sit comfortably in a young child's vocabulary.

What, When, Why & What's Happening

The command needs to find a target and register with others - (what needs doing) 'Get Help' (when) 'NOW' (why) 'this is a stranger' (what's he doing) 'trying to take them away'. Teaching these skills to children are highly beneficial, and if practised they become second nature or a way of communicating when they are in difficulty.

Part of my role has been auditing communication and I have had to listen to many 999 calls from children, I am sure this would make a difference in all areas when they are communicating *their need* for help.

An example of a recent Ambulance call from a child took five minutes to find out that his parent had lost consciousness and may have been attacked. It started something like this:

An Example of an Emergency Call

"Hello - I've just got in from school and I couldn't find my mum, then I went in the kitchen, I have found her now, but she is asleep on the floor",

"Okay caller what's your name and how old are you"

" my name is Peter and I'm twelve"

"Okay Peter, why is your mum on the floor?"

"I don't know , I think I.......I know I just found her there when I came in the kitchen"

"Can you see if she is breathing?"

"Yeah, I think she is" – (not certain)

" Can you see her though? - tell me what you can see?"

"Yes...I can see her, but she is sort of......half under the table"

"Has she been drinking? Does she have any health problems?"

"No – she hasn't been drinking and she is normally Ok"

"Okay Peter, I want you to go over to her, put your ear next to her mouth and tell me if you can hear, or feel her breathing"

"I don't think I can.... I mean.... she is laying on her face....its down..... and there is blood on the floor around her head".

It has taken three minutes to find this out and a further two minutes for Peter to give his address at the start of the call. He lives in a new road and doesn't know his postcode. An ambulance would have been dispatched at this point 5 minutes into the call.

Being a clinical call coach has allowed me to practice numerous times in different scenarios. The longest, similar type of call I have had to audit, took 14 minutes to find out that a baby was breathing, but not conscious. Communicating in an emergency needs to be brief, uncomplicated and be able to withstand probability.

The in-experienced call handler was reading Peter's probability, his mum was probably okay. It probably wasn't serious. Allowing him to continue answering in open-ended questions, when he wasn't sure, was a mistake, and didn't get to the root of the problem quick enough. Practice, Practice and more Practice........

Teach Them How to Use a Telephone, What to Say & Make a Script

Keep the numbers and a script on the wall near the telephone, or nearby. Let them write the script out – it will embed easier that way, colour code it for, use a traffic light system that is easy to understand. You wouldn't want them calling the police because the cat didn't come home last night.....It happens... and it's not always children. A man rang 999 for the Fire Brigade, to ask if he could borrow one of their ladders!. Red for emergencies and you can run through some scenarios.

The local non-emergency number for Amber and a neighbour or relative close by for Green.

If they are young or it is a new handset, teach them how to use it. Teach them what they need to say, remembering that if it was a Red emergency then they might need to communicate in a different way. Give them scenarios that you read out and get them to relay back to you, the important points in priority. If they then happen on a an emergency, at home or out and about, they will know what to assess and what to relay.

Children are now being taught resuscitation in schools, run through this with them. They may need to perform it on a sibling or friend, or you. How are they going to use the phone then?. Where is the loud speaker on the phone?, how can they turn the volume up and down?.

Teach Them to Scatter

There is a rather horrible and sad account of a woman pedestrian out with her two children. They were aged about six and nine. She is approached by a man in a busy high street who starts to verbally abuse her. He is not known to the family. The woman tries to side step him and go around him. The children don't know what to do and the youngest grips the back of her coat. In the scuffle that broke out the child is dragged around on the back of her coat and is hit against a parked car and the pavement several times. While the older child is stood crying and witness to the whole event. It was a case of mistaken identity on the part of the delusional and angry man, and this is not as rare an occurrence as you might think.

Protect them from being and seeing hurt.

Teaching children to scatter, is to protect them.

Teach them where to go, what to say, where to get help and to keep out of the way. Use a special word so that they know you mean business. Teach them this in the house too. Where should they go, or where could they hide and how could they summon help. Have a plan in place, tag it onto the end of your what to do 'if there was a fire in the house' routine, give them a chance to practice it, time them. Reward them for it.

Teach Them to Chose Well, When Finding Someone to Help Them

This may seem obvious but the world has changed. The survey revealed that some parents were taught to look for a policeman if they got into any difficulty. This is now, not as easy as it seems. Then, they were taught as a child, to go and ask an adult for help. They were, however, not taught how to choose a suitable adult in a crowd. My advice to my children has been to look for a family. I also describe what a family should look like. There are many interpretations of family and you need to be specific when asking them who they would choose.

If you walk them to school, run through some scenarios with them, ask them to point out which of the houses or buildings they would choose to go to, and why. If you think you can do better or you are concerned by their choices, then you can point some out and say why you think these would be better.

It is not easy to imagine them going from the 'frying pan to the fire', but it could happen. Running up to someone with a dog might be a visible deterrent, but not if the dog then attacks them. If they run and hide under a car that then drives away or doesn't see them, it's not a good outcome. If where they run to is isolated and then nobody is home, they are just more vulnerable. Teach them to look for open public places.

If my child had a problem on the high street I would tell him that if he had no choice then he should run into a pub. Go behind the bar, Lock-On to something, the Landlord would soon ring the Police. It is about getting them to make quick choices running into a church hall might be an over seventies aerobics class or it might just be a Judo Club.....Result.

Your Child's File

No parent would ever want to feel that they live in a society where they would need to keep a file, but times have changed. This type of dossier is becoming more common in America and the advice is, that we should be doing it here.

What Should be Kept in it?

Photo – Keep a full, front on, head and shoulders picture of your child. Keep it up to date by replacing it annually. Keep their hair off their face and if they wear glasses you should have two pictures, one with and one without.

Dental Records – Know where your child's dental records are kept, if your child has a dental X-Ray, ask your dentist for a copy and keep it in their file.

Description – Keep a written, up to date description of your child and their characteristics, anything that they do that is specific to them, thumb sucking, hair twiddling, and nail biting are all good examples. This might seem odd, but in the panic of having to report a missing child, it is precisely these little details that make the difference, but might not be remembered at the time. They do make a difference, an example might be looking for a child on CCTV at an airport. Passing on habitual information may assist someone's ability to pick them out of a crowd..

Distinguishing Marks – Birthmarks, scars, deformities, quirks - one of my children had very wide feet, for his entire childhood, and required special order, wide fitting shoes.

Medication – Keep a list of any long-term, regularly taken medication, its trade name and what it is used for, how many doses and when. What happens if they do not have it. Any other specific instructions – if it is a medication that they might carry with them. Discuss with your child what this medication does and what it is for – if they carry an inhaler, insulin or an Epipen. For older children - this could be one of their 'use what you have' – tools. Give them your permission to use it, when to use it, how to use it and what might happen to someone else if they do.

Finger Prints - Unique to your child and update them every couple of years as your child grows. Do it for the whole family so that your child doesn't feel singled out in a process that is not an every day, every child, activity. The finger printing kits can be bought on the internet.

What to do With The File.

Keep this file safe and out of reach, let them decorate the front if you want to make them feel involved. If you ever needed this information, it is ready and you are not going to be in a fit state, or have the ability to be methodical at that time. Make your spouse or partner aware of it, tell grandparents where it is kept.

The Working it Out - Together – Work Books:

These books are specifically designed for an adult to work through, with a child. They are age appropriate in one book and there are exercises to work through up until the age of twelve. There is a different book for teenagers, it is designed in a communication style that is in short bursts and has tasks for them to demonstrate their skills and abilities. All of the above key, teaching points and more are discussed and presented in more detail in these work books. They are an excellent resource.

Sometimes it makes a difference to have a work book and rather than appear to be nagging a pre-teen, you are allowing them to demonstrate that they have the skills to be out for an hour later or go to the cinema with their friends. The work books are critical thinking in demonstration, scenario based and have moral reasoning and judgement tests, presented in an age appropriate style. They assist you with keeping your child close and engaged. They have short exercises and some that require a more reflective input on their part. They are available at a cost that covers printing and postage only and are a not-for-profit resource. You can access them soon on our website.

Good Luck – Remember it is Your Gift, to them.

Don't Let Them Forget You.

Keep your children engaged with you and family life – there is one common feature of missing children and those that are cyber abused and that is:

They become disengaged from their family life in some way.

Value them and their safety and teach them well; a family code word, a special whistle, gift them with survival techniques and stories that will matter to them and these in turn will be passed on to their children, all because of you, all because you took the time.

Don't Leave Them Alone on a Dark Day.

This is a difficult one and one that I probably have a 'heads up' on but that's not what's important here anyone can do this and it's a real gift.

Health Warning:
Don't read this on a day when you are sad, lonely or anxious...It won't help at all.

It is very important to me that my children are not left alone on a dark day. If something terrible happens to one of my children and there is no way out for them then this is my final gift. It takes time and it takes practice but it's my final investment in their childhood. If their childhood was brought to an end this is what I would want for them.

There are benefits too. One of my children stopped developing Migraines after this and stopped being anxious about doing new things. It helps children Fly,

Take Exams, Speak Publicly, Have a Voice and Perform Better at School and in Interviews so its potential is not limited; but if a dark day came and I could not get to them in time or I didn't know where they were this is what I have gifted them..

Why it's Important to Every Parent and Every Child

In my practice I have worked with some parents who have lost a child, the example I am going to use is that of a mother who lost her son. The insights she gave me have gone on to inform and shape my practice with other parents today.

It was a normal midweek morning in the busy household of the Greys', five children all getting ready for school and nursery. The eldest son had a test that day and wanted to leave early to meet up with a friend and revise. He left taking a piece of toast off of one of the younger children's plates, they started squealing and an argument broke out. The mum in the household clipped the older boy around the head before wishing him good luck on his test; she then proceeded to make more toast for the tearfully wronged toast less child. She then dropped off three children at school, a short distance from the house, and continued to walk on to the nursery for the youngest Grey.

Her journey through the London streets that day was particularly noisy there seemed to be sirens sounding every couple of minutes an ambulance flew past and then another and then a police car; it was a busy London morning.

When she got home she put the kettle on, it was now time for her to have some breakfast and she sat with a coffee and a piece of toast while she watched TV in the kitchen. She would then need to load the dishwasher and spend the rest of the day with her companion, the washing machine. As she sat drinking her final sips of coffee there was a knock at the door. It was probably her neighbour, she often came in and watched TV or had a coffee. Mrs Grey went to answer the door.

At the door stood two police officers with their hats removed. Mrs Grey said she knew immediately that something was wrong. The officers came into the kitchen and told her that her eldest son had been knocked down by a van on the way to school that morning and that he was in a critical condition. He had been air lifted to hospital and that she would need to come with them, they would take her to him but she needed to leave now.

Mrs Grey left the TV on and everything as it was, she put on a pair of her husbands shoes she remembers that she couldn't find her own and they left. The police car raced through the streets of London, sirens blasting. It was at this point that Mrs Grey asked the police officer what time the accident had happened. She knew that the ambulances she had seen that morning were probably racing to her son who had been knocked down just 200 yards from the house. She sat the rest of the journey in a quiet reflective silence.

When she got to the hospital she remembers the looks that she got from the staff as she walked the long length of the ward, they seemed to look at her and then look away. She was led into a room with the blinds closed and there was her son, laying still, The doctor who was stood at his bedside reached out to Mrs Grey with both arms as if to catch her, and said "I'm so sorry.........he's just gone".

I saw Mrs Grey because she was stuck, riddled with guilt and anxiety she couldn't function. She knew she had a good husband and four other children and had to get on; but she was just stuck. She could not get past feeling guilty. Guilty for not getting there in time, or not bothering to see what the sirens were about that day or that she hadn't kissed him goodbye that morning. But most of all she was stuck because he had been conscious for an hour after the accident, for 45 minutes he had been laying on the cold road just 200 yards from her, with all this commotion going on around him, his leg had been trapped under the van, freeing him would have been noisy, he would have been frightened, he would have wanted her and she wasn't there.

She spent countless hours of every day at the kitchen table starring into empty space wondering if he had been in pain, if he had said anything, did he cry, did anyone comfort him? It was a torture that she could not escape from. Many months passed and Mrs Grey stopped going out, people stopped coming around and then she stopped sleeping, eating or talking.

When I first saw Mrs Grey she told me that her son would have told her off if he'd of seen her like that. With some help Mrs Grey came back in her own time and the last I heard was she regularly pinches a piece of toast of the younger children's plates... just to remind her of her son, but it is a common theme for parents that lose a child to spend a lot of time feeling the pain of those last minutes or hours if they cannot be there. If they cannot get to their children. Imagine then the torture of Ann Downey, Mrs Dowler, Denise Bulger and the Dads too. Kevin Wells' book *Goodbye, Dearest Holly as* an example.

As parents we never know when a 'Grey Day' is coming and the gift I give to my children is a double gift. It is for them and it is for me.

The Anchor Technique

This requires practice and needs to be practised at least ten times to be effective. It will then need regular visits to keep it alive. This is a Neuro-Linguistic Technique that will imprint on them and provide them with a place to go – just before an exam, a flight on an aeroplane or a special interview/entrance exam or other.

This is What You Will Need:

You need quiet and your child, one to one, and one at a time.

……..

They need to lay with their eyes closed, somewhere that is familiar to them, their bedroom on their own bed, or on the sofa in their own home.

…...

Younger children, with their eyes closed, may appreciate you touching them on their forehead to reassure them or help them to relax – older children & teenagers would prefer you didn't – in my experience.

…...

Use a voice that is clear but relaxed.

…...

Ask them to remember a time in their life when they felt really happy – get them to describe it.

How it made them feel – you want them to feel that now, you want them to relive that memory, now and in full colour.

…...

Get them to describe what they can see, hear, smell and feel, is the sun on their face?

Can they hear birds singing? Or

Maybe they are at their first ever football match they hear the crowd chant, they can smell chips, they can see steam rising off the pitch.

Their favourite player walks on the pitch and the crowd erupts....wow

......

You want this film to play in their mind, to be vivid in detail, you need them to be there to create the same feelings, in them.

......

when they are really feeling these feelings, they should have a relaxed face or a slight smile.

When they are really there, then ask them to stay there, in that moment, soaking up those feelings.

....

You then ask them to pinch together their thumb and second finger (on their non-dominant hand) get them to do this while they relive their happiest moment, at its highest peak.

....

By doing this, you are creating an anchor. anchoring feelings of relaxation and happiness, linked to a physical action, They use their non-dominant hand so that any decision to return to this state is a deliberate one and cannot be made by mistake.

......

Remember

Timing is critical, you want them to be able to anchor these feelings, when they are at their peak.

With practice, they will have instant access to a state of mind that is highly desirable and able to crush even the most ingrained nerves. Get them to practice this regularly and they will be in very good company. The thumb and second finger technique is commonly used by athletes, so make a game of it, next time they are watching runners prepare for a race or any athlete, get them to look for physical signs of anchoring – when you know what to look for it is surprising who you might see using this technique – but athletes have been using it for years.

When they have mastered the technique – don't be surprised if you find they are calmer, sleeping better and performing better. Once you have helped them master this then you are ready to help them reach the next level. Or the gift you would want them to have if you couldn't get to them in time or they were alone, in a very dire situation. Always remember why you are doing this, as it may not sit easy with you – but it is a gift for both of you.

Their Own Private Sanctuary

In this technique, you will set it up in the same way, ask them to use their anchor technique to fully relax. Then you will, together, set up a sanctuary. It is imperative that you give it some thought before you start. Think about what is important to them – if they are into Ballet, Football or Horses it will play a part.

They are going to create a place to go, I chose to use a garden for my children. It is a secluded garden that is surrounded by a ten foot wall, my younger son has a football pitch in his, my older child has a wildlife sanctuary in his and my father, who passed away recently, stays on and tends to tall the animals that live there. So you can see anything goes.

There has to be a specific entrance to their place and it will involve a short journey to get there, this is to prepare them and ensure that they always enter their sanctuary fully relaxed. So here we go...................

The Entrance to the Sanctuary

They enter a room, if they are into football we will use this as an example, but change it to suit your child's interests. They enter the room and all the football team are there. They greet him with a smile and clap, after all, he is 'man of the match'.

The walls are all painted red and there are tables covered in red cloth, that sweeps to the floor. The tables that are on three sides of the room, against the walls, are covered in trophies and they all belong to your child and his team. Tell him to walk over to them and touch them, feel the cool marble plinths that they stand on.

Make the room as real as you can and describe it to them, from their suggestions.

At the other end of the room is a door made of glass and outside is a small private patio area. Smiling to his friends he walks over to the door and opens it. He goes out onto the patio and there in front of him are some stone steps with a gold handrail that spirals down out of sight. He should now walk over to the steps. There are ten steps and they are lit up with lights to show the way.

He starts slowly to walk down the steps and you count them out for him, your voice is calm and you count them down as he goes. When he gets to the bottom step, you describe a door in-front of him and It is a big heavy door – it has a big lock on it, he has the key in his pocket. On the floor, by the door is a box with a big chain around it, and it has a letter box opening at the top. Here he can post any worries that are bothering him (don't ask what these are, they are private and must remain so). He takes the key out of his pocket and turns it in the lock.

Going Inside his Sanctuary

On the first session, you will be required to assist

your child in building up their sanctuary and you need to give them ideas and suggestions. But do remember it is there place and this is not a space for you to demonstrate your interior decorating skills – this belongs to them and anything goes.

When they push open the door, you can describe it as heavy, needing a lot of effort. They close the door and it's then that they will need your help to suggest what should be inside their sanctuary.

Here is an example of what we did – he opens the door and standing behind it is my dad, who hugs him and squeezes him tight, they close the door and begin to walk around the sanctuary. There is a large weeping willow tree and under that is a bench, they sit down on the bench and a small deer comes out of the undergrowth around the tree. My son leans forward on the bench to stroke it. The deer's fur feels warm from the sun, soft and silky. The deer stays just for a few moments and then leaves. Other animals are walking freely around the sanctuary and my son and his grandad sit talking on the bench. My son now feels highly relaxed, safe and with his family.

With practice, their sanctuary can be accessed in seconds, the routine becomes embedded in the mind and simply, appearing in their minds eye at the top of the stair case, is enough to begin the journey down the ten steps. Anything goes in their place, anything that makes them feel relaxed. There should be a family member and it should have some sort of surround and safety. It could be in a castle, or a secret cave, on a favourite beach, the theme should always have steps down to it, as it needs to be a recognised step and a conscious decision to go there. If they need to get up and move quickly they can, this is merely a state of mind and a state of trained relaxation. This is not hypnosis or something that will dull their senses if they need to react.

Great Rewards Await Those Who Practice.......I Can Promise You.

What is the Significance of This Gift

This gift has given my children the ability to cope and I have told them that if ever I can not get to them, in time – or at all, if they need to feel safe and they are alone, frightened or feeling pain – they can instantly transport themselves to their sanctuary. There, a family member will be waiting for them, and will love them, hold them and support them, until I can get there.

If I cant get to them, then I will know where to find them. I will know that they were with, in their minds eye, a trusted and much loved relative. I will remember them there - feeding a deer and soaking up the sun on their face.

Remember that this is a skill for life and they can feed their deer's and soak up their sun or hug their relatives - just before surgery, a big exam, a speech or a performance of some kind. It reduces stress, encourages deeper sleep and relaxes both the conscious and subconscious mind. It truly is a gift of unmeasurable gain.

Happy Parenting, Happy Days

Chapter Seventeen

The, "It's Time" – Campaign

"What you absolutely, positively have to do and do now.....it's time"

Knowing what we now know about the risks to our children and that the cover ups will likely continue, then we surely know............it's time.

There is a Call to Action

There is a forgotten force in this equation, a quiet army of foot soldiers already on the ground. Already primed with the unique ability to do the job of protection and who could do the job well.

Parents, Grand Parents & Step Parents

It is every parents responsibility to protect today's children in our current climate. They have been forgotten, left out of the equation, dropped from the agenda and abused by the very people who profess to protect them. Labelled as 'throwaways' and a 'lost generation'. Parents labelled as 'feckless' in a Broken Britain that now appears not to have a hope in hell of recovering its dignity, prosperity or its affinity to its young.

Set up watchers, be a doer and not a looker, there is no place for bystanders, or ne'er-do-wells, no room for error. There is no place for the silent or the secretive, there should be no more stories of children eating from bird tables or sobbing in alleyways, without action or without question. No child should be the toy of the rich, or the victim of the cruel, just because we pretend we cannot see them. If they are hungry, forgotten or alone, we must act to protect them and then follow up that it is done. Children are not carers or keepers of society they are here to explore it, contribute to, and change it, for the better. If they are allowed to care about the world they live in, they will see it as theirs, their responsibility and their gift to others.

The time is now, how will you act? What will you do? When will you do it?

Make one small change at a time.
Let yourself get used to it, embed it.
Then make another, and another, and another.
Share your ideas with others, get your ideas from your children.

Club together and make a 'go to the cinema' night, make a group of wardens for a safe walk to school route, make a park play date once a month with other parents, If you run a group, make sure all the children are picked up safely, know who has to walk home alone, and help them. Make a to-don't list for your group or club, or school, or circle of friends.

Don't confuse caring with interfering – the outcomes are different

Which type of person are you? The one who finds a child's hat in the street and then hangs it on a fence nearby, in the hope that they might find it,

or

Do you just step over it?

Is it time to be different, or time to help others to be different?

To do nothing, to say nothing is to be nothing

"Sometimes I would watch her from the window, it was just after I put the bread out for the birds, she would come over and eat it all"
Victoria Clumbie's Neighbour

Stand Up, Speak Up, Don't Give Up

"He would come up to my room when my parents were out, he smelt of drink, he would climb on top of me, under my bed clothes, he would always reach in his

pocket afterwards and put some sweets under my pillow, One day my mother asked me what this stain was on my bedding when she was doing the laundry. I began to tell her and then she cried"
Katy, aged 11

A Closing Word From the Author

Let me know how you're doing, what you think might help.
Let me know if you need help, ideas or contacts
Check the website regularly for - trusted contact

**email me at
contact@rubyfrench37@yahoo.com
Good Luck, you can make it happen – it's time**

Chapter Eighteen

An Open Letter to David Cameron PM

**An Open Letter to PM David Cameron
February, 2014**

Dear PM Cameron,
**A Prime Minister, without, Government is nothing and not,
A Prime Minister, without Government, is nothing**
 I, like many UK parents, voted for you because we believed you stood for the former, rather than the latter.

Please do not let us down, we are tired, we are sometimes hungry and often cold, in the homes we struggle to pay for, but we are not stupid, we are not silent and we are not without collective opinion. We to, can collaborate, we to, can collude. Let us do this, in support of you, and not in spite of you. Show us that you care, show us that,
'Every Child Matters'
We want action, we want it now, because we want to believe in you.

We want you to secure and agree a UK wide definition on child abduction.

We want child abduction recorded and counted by every police force in the country.

We want an adult friendly, annual, reported figure on child abduction in the UK.

We want workable, practical, child safety advice, that is measured to be effective.

We want other countries to look to Britain as the lead on child protection.

We want the 'the one-stop-shop' for access to information, as promised to parents.

Yours sincerely
Disillusioned, despondent and downright dejected,
Britain.

The End,
Or is it just the Start?

"The most common way people give up their power
is by thinking they don't have any"
Alice Walker, Author, Poet, and Activist

www.ingramcontent.com/pod-product-compliance
Lightning Source LLC
Chambersburg PA
CBHW022108090426
42743CB00008B/768